# PERCY'S WAR

## D-Day memories of Coronation Street's Bill Waddington

## BY STAFFORD HILDRED

*wordstar*
PUBLISHING

# FOREWORD

Bill Waddington landed on the beaches of Normandy shortly after D-Day. Ever since his days with Stars in Battle Dress, to now becoming the famed Percy Sugden in Coronation Street, he has been a loyal supporter of Army charities.

It is wonderful news that profits from the sale of this book will be given to the Army's Central Charity - The Army Benevolent Fund. We are most grateful to Bill for this and wish him and the book every success.

GENERAL SIR BRIAN KENNY GCB CBE
Chairman
The Army Benevolent Fund

Published by
Wordstar Publishing,
Littlefield,
Church Street,
Tansley,
Matlock,
Derbyshire,
England DE4 5FE.

First published in Great Britain in 1994.

ISBN: 1 898926 00 X

British Library Cataloguing-in-Publication Data: A catalogue record
for this book is available from the British Library.

Cover design by Trevor Gillies, Nottingham.
Typesetting & Production by Writers Media Services, Nottingham.
Printed and bound in Great Britain by BDC Printing Services, Derby.

# CONTENTS

# *Back to the Front*

It took me nearly 50 years to return to the beaches of Normandy. There were so many memories and emotions tied up with that bleak French coastline. So many young comrades were cruelly cut down within days, or even hours, of landing that somehow it never seemed quite the right time to go back.

Almost half a century later, before the ceremonies and services turn the anniversary into an 'event', I wanted to make a quiet, low-key journey back down my personal memory lane. The purpose of my trip was to pay my own small tribute to the men who did not return.

The 50th anniversary is such a colossal landmark that I knew I had to go. I was apprehensive of course, but before the ceremonies and the speeches began I wanted to see how half a century had changed the landscape that saw the War finally tip in the favour of the Allies.

I didn't really think how much it might upset me or know what it would take out of me if I went, I just knew I had to privately salute all the men who did not come back. It was the only way I could express my feelings.

It was a sad and moving experience, as I

knew it would be. But it was also uplifting, because I could reminisce on the happier moments of wartime as well as the tragedies and reflect on how fortunate we are to still enjoy the peace that so many men gave their lives to achieve. I am always conscious that I have enjoyed 50 extra years of life that were denied to so many men. After that you've got to owe them something even if it's a debt than can never be paid.

The second time in my life that I went to the Normandy beaches was earlier this year and the first thing I noticed was how much everything had changed. The beaches themselves were just as I remembered them but this time they seemed so quiet and empty. In early June 1944 the beach at Arromanches, where I landed among a contingent of Scots Guards, was packed with milling troops, heavy equipment and the air was full of noise, shells screaming overhead, shouted orders and intermittent gunfire. It was all at the same time totally terrifying and inescapably exciting.

I was surprised to see how much remained of the old landing craft both on the beach and in the shallow water. I like to think the French appreciate the reminders of D-Day that began the long battle to free their country from the German invaders.

But as soon as we moved inland while the flat farmland looked familiar the buildings looked so different. The green and fertile countryside is unchanged although we didn't have much time for sight-seeing the first time around, everything moved so fast. You had your mind firmly fixed on self-preservation and doing your job. So we were never long enough in a place to get to know it. If you stayed in one place for a week it was an awfully long time.

Although I had prepared myself for the experience I was still almost overwhelmed when I went into the British Cemetery at Bayeux. The beautifully tended grass and the long lines of white gravestones was exactly what I expected yet the messages on the gravestones were still deeply disturbing. So many of the British soldiers were just so young. Seventeen, eighteen and nineteen year olds, it breaks my heart to think of their lives ending while mine was allowed to go on. They never really had a life.

I found one grave, of 'An Unknown British Soldier' who fell on June 10, 1944. That was my own 28th birthday. And somehow that plain white gravestone brought my own good fortune rushing home to me. I stood quietly for a long time and looked at that grave and tried to pay my respects to all the brave lads who did not come back.

That is why I made the trip and that is why I'm writing this book. I'm 77 now and fast approaching my 78th birthday as I write. I've enjoyed a full and happy life. I was fortunate to be given the talent to amuse and entertain and the War first gave me the chance to use that talent.

I've gone from stage and radio success with a Royal Variety Performance on the way to a long late run in the best television series in the world. I've been able to earn a tremendous living doing a job I love. I've been wonderfully happily married and sadly left alone. But I've never experienced anything in my life like the feeling of sailing across the English Channel with the certain knowledge that the most fearsome fighting force the world has ever known was waiting to blow the life out of me and mine.

So I took my journey slowly. I stood for a long time on the beach at Arromanches. A few sea-gulls and a brace of early morning fishermen were all I had for company, and all I wanted.

Firmly gripped by my memories I determined to retrace as many of my wartime steps as I could. In 1944 the ride to the little village of Sommerview had seemed quite an expedition.

This time the few kilometres passed in a trice and I explored the scene of our first stop. But the old monastery where we first made camp has long gone in a wave of post-war redevelopment so I pressed on to Bayeux.

In 1944 the home of the famous tapestry was one of the first towns to be freed. It was taken from the surprised Germans without a battle. The British Cemetery was a difficult emotional experience for me. It was very, very nostalgic for me in there. I looked at those graves and I just knew I could so easily have been in one of them. Opposite the Cemetery is a wartime museum. I'm not sure whether it was my age or the Normandy Veteran's badge that is proudly worn on my blazer but I was waved inside without charge.

The bureaucratic madame in charge of the collection of uniforms and other military memorabilia seemed deeply concerned lest I shoot a photograph. I thought of saying that her kinsfolk had welcomed the British shooting when I arrived 50 years previously, but the lady was but a child then and I let it pass.

The pictures of the bombing of nearby Caen were to me the most memorable parts of the collection. I watched that historic onslaught from a hill some 15 miles away as wave after wave of Allied bombers flattened the city that was proving a real stumbling block to the advance.

The Germans had mainly already moved out but we had to attack the city to prevent them from coming back. As I walked round Caen it had all the signs of a bustling modern city but, if you look a bit deeper, you can still see the pock-marked walls where our bombs left their mark.

It was still hard to reconcile the smouldering ruin I drove into in July 1944 with the thriving community that exists today. But in the splendid Peace Museum is a comprehensive recollection of the cruel struggle of 50 years ago.

I found the details of the conflict quite fascinating but as I sit with my thoughts in quiet reflection I realise I am not trying to write a history book. Far more learned folk than myself have recorded every raid and every skirmish of that dreadful War.

My story is a personal one, of a chirpy lad from Lancashire whose life was totally changed by the fortunes of war. The experience became my passport to a career as an entertainer, it gave me the chance to make something of myself and of the talents I was given.

It is dedicated to all those brothers in arms who did not get that chance. As I quietly toured round the battlefields of Normandy I kept pinching myself to remind me how lucky I was to be able to travel all those memory lanes.

Nowadays millions of faithful Coronation Street viewers watch Percy Sugden's honest efforts to keep alive the values of an old soldier in a changing world. Certainly he's pompous and inclined to pontificate but, maybe because I've shared so many experiences with the old boy, I find myself agreeing with what he has to say more and more.

My strongest memories of the War are of the camaraderie. Even the word sounds old-fashioned these days but to me there is no better feeling than being part of a group of trusted pals. The brotherhood between us was fantastic. You knew that these men would do anything for you and you would do anything for them. Thrown together by the circumstances of war we simply got on with it. I met men from the most upper crust of families and I met men whose families scratched a living as rag and bone men. All of a sudden in wartime those distinctions did not matter. We were all in the same boat.

There were blokes who would have been definite wrong-uns in normal life who received from their participation in the War a purpose and a feeling of belonging that is sadly missing from so many areas of our society today. I'm certainly not in favour of another war, but the call to arms did have a mightily positive effect on many of my comrades. Once they were given some responsibility they rose to the challenge.

The War was a great leveller and it lead to an enormous instant increase in understanding of how other people had to live their lives. People with privilege realised how lucky they were. People with nothing learned that all toffs were not so special underneath. The War was a hard school but it provided an invaluable education.

It made us pull together in a way that is

hard to comprehend these days. Nobody had very much and if you had a cigarette it was simply expected that you would split it in two and share it with a pal.

Not that we could ever get cigarettes. One of my earliest jokes was to go up to the back of a crowd and ask: "What are we all waiting for? Are they going to bring a packet of fags past here in half an hour?"

I used to go into the bank and say: "Can I have 20 Players?" When they looked astonished at my request I would explain that I couldn't get them anywhere else so I might as well try there.

And even if you got them they were almost impossible to smoke. There was one brand called Pasha which was absolutely terrible. I never did find out which stable they got that stuff out of. Red Ten were pretty awful as well. I think cigarettes like that did more to stop people smoking than any Government health warning.

We really were healthier then. People were much fitter during the War. We were all rationed to two ounces of butter a week, two ounces of sugar, maybe a quarter of a pound of meat. Everyone looked so much better for it than they look today. You could live quite well on the ration. As soon as it was lifted people started to gorge themselves and you began to see these peculiar looking square-shaped people. It's just greed, plain and simple.

I was 11 stone 3lb at 21 and now I'm 12 stone 3lb. If I cut out the whisky for a month or two I would be back to my original weight, but I would miss it too much.

Those early days in France made me grow up in a hurry. As the comedian in an entertainment party from Stars in Battle-Dress we were hurtling around in our lorry from makeshift theatre to the next temporary stage and we passed everything in the way of human tragedy from bombed out houses to corpses lying where they fell.

My job was to try to make people forget about the War as much as I could. It pleases me enormously when people come up and recall having seen me in France. One chap from Leicester stopped me outside Coronation Street only recently and told me, 'I'll never forget laughing at you on the Normandy Beaches. It took our minds right off all the horrors. We were talking about you for a month after you had gone. I tingled all over when he told me that. It's a wonderful feeling to think that you've done something useful.

At times I felt I was lucky not to be right up at the sharpest end of all the fighting, but then a shell would whizz over and land nearby or we would have to dodge gingerly out of a minefield and I realised that no-one was safe in Normandy in 1944.

Humour is a very powerful weapon. And I believe it is Britain's greatest strength. That is why our nation is so difficult to defeat. We can laugh at adversity and that is a crucial release valve for emotion that allows us to see the funny side and then battle on.

I think that was never more important than in the darkest days of the War. And it was one of the key differences between Britain and her enemies. You never heard the Germans laughing at themselves! If the Germans had had a national sense of humour they would never have been ruled by Hitler in the first place.

They'd have laughed at the idea of a nutcase taking power and never got him in charge in the first place, the silly sod.

All that Achtung and Donner und Blitzen nonsense. You can't imagine British swallowing that lunacy.

Now I am proud of my row of medals,

although the only one I actually won was for boxing. The rest were awarded for 'being there'. I didn't claim my medals at the end of the War. An old Colonel I know asked me long afterwards: "Did you get your War medals, Bill?"

I said: "No. I was pleased enough to get home in one piece, I never thought about claiming them." He offered to do it for me so I told him everywhere I had been and he organised it for me.

Eventually they arrived with a bill for £25. I said: "I thought I had won all these, I didn't realise I would have to pay for them." But they are dress medals and I'm still very proud of them.

As I searched modern Normandy for landmarks of the War I had my nostalgic moments. I suppose it was a sentimental journey and sometimes, looking out to sea from the hills above Arromanches for once, I almost thought I heard a stirring broadcast from Winston Churchill.

When you consider how politicians are regarded today it must be hard for younger people to appreciate how Churchill was revered. He led this nation so brilliantly well in the last War and he should never be forgotten.

The sound of one of his stirring speeches coming crackling out of one of those big old radios we had in those days really used to make the hairs on the back of your neck stand up.

I believe he was the greatest man who ever walked. A hero, if ever there was one. He was inspirational. Even in our most difficult days, when this country stood alone against Hitler's victory he still made you feel as though we would win in the end.

Patriotism might not be a very popular emotion these days and even then there was the odd carping voice. I was on leave once in London relaxing in a pub when Churchill came on the radio. That emotive voice began to get into his stride and everyone was hushed into respectful silence apart from three young blokes who had probably drunk more than was good for them. they talked above Churchill and without a word about six of us moved forward and propelled that disrespectful trio swiftly out of the door.

The thing was that no-one ever believed it was going to last that long. People were boldly saying, 'Come on lads, let's join up. It'll be over by Christmas. It was only later when they began to wonder, 'Which Christmas?'

It was an amazing six years. We had a lot of setbacks, but I believe that 'comes the hour comes the man'. We had some very, very brave young men that when it came to it were determined to fight for their country. That British spirit should never be underestimated. They weren't bullied into it, they went in with great heart.

And while the American soldiers would talk to their officers as though they were next door neighbours, we didn't have that in our Army. We had total respect. I found the majority of our officers were well educated and well trained and I never found it difficult to behave properly. Most people were the same. There is enormous strength in that discipline. If you tried to get clever, you were in trouble.

But if you were late back off leave all you had to say was, 'I had to come through Birmingham, sir,' and usually they understood. I still have problems with that city's road system. I almost think it was easier when we took the signposts down in case the Germans landed.

Humour was always my weapon. I remember just after I joined up a soldier was writing home to his wife and he asked someone how to spell Hitler. H..I..T..E..R came the reply. Where is the L? asked the soldier. We've just knocked that out of him, was the joke.

And visiting Normandy again reminded me of the time the Luftwaffe was said to have handed out tinned milk to our pilots in a vain attempt to keep them off Brest. They were corny gags, even then. But they caught the mood of the moment and helped soldiers to release their tension.

For the first three weeks after I landed in Normandy I cannot honestly remember sleeping at all. I was simply terrified. Shells were going over us in both directions almost all the time and I suppose I thought my number was bound to come up sooner or later.

It wasn't until after I'd had a wild night out with a cousin of mine in Bayeux that alcohol and exhaustion took over and my mind and body really came to terms with my new surroundings.

The noise was still horrendous most of the time but someone told me: "The one you don't hear is the one that hits you," and afterwards I stopped worrying about the deafening noise so much.

So many of the buildings were flattened or

badly damaged by the fighting that it's hard to retrace your steps. After 50 years I could not find any trace of the Casino in the seaside town of Lion-sur-Mer.

Mind you, that was in a bad state even then. It was bombed out when I did one of my first shows there in June 1944. Our Commandos had been ahead of us and they had really done the Germans over. There was only half a roof left on. Halfway through the show there was an enormous bang.

Everyone flinched, and I just managed to say: "It's all right. I think the Russians have arrived." They laughed so loud, and the place was so dilapidated I was very worried that for once I was going to bring the house down in more ways than one.

Afterwards when we came out we found out what had happened. A little old French gardener, trying to bring some normality back among all the conflict, had been trimming the hedge outside what had been the old German headquarters and he had triggered a huge booby trap bomb. He was blown to bits and there were many other casualties as well. Remarkably we got used to things like that. You soon realised you couldn't be upset all the time.

My job was to make people forget their troubles.

The powers that be realised that the men needed some diversion from the horrors of War then it would benefit them. And it did. They made a wonderful audience these lads and they gave me confidence to cut out a lot of the funny make-ups I used to use. I only brought them in to give me confidence. If you look funny you feel funny, I thought. But gradually I realised I did not need the props so much, so long as the gags were up to scratch. As the War went on I relied less on outlandish outfits.

Although one of my favourites was a skit on an upper class twit of an officer Major de Vere Farquharson-Farquharson, Bart the inventor of the Nissen hut, dressed like a Major with a monocle.

After the war when I started work for Moss Empires I went through the same thing again. I lacked confidence to entertain ordinary members of the public. I knew soldiers and how to make them laugh because I was one. But when it came to re-launching in Civvy Street I went right back to silly make-up. Soon the message came down from on high. Bill Waddington is very funny. He doesn't need that daft get-up.

There are many astonishing things that have happened to me in my life. But the way those talented writers at Coronation Street came up with the experiences of Percy Sugden that have parallels in my real-life, without knowing anything about my life, never fails to amaze me.

To start with, when I got the part, even I didn't know that my own great-grandmother was called Sugden. So how could they know? Then they had Percy recalling his wartime exploits with The Cookhouse Follies, before ever any of them knew that I actually was in Britain's first World War Two concert party The Blue Pencils and that I really did spend some time in the cookhouse.

The only aspect of Percy Sugden's wartime exploits that does not coincide with mine was his time in Africa as a Desert Rat. It was John Stephenson, one of my favourite writers, who came up with the immortal Percy Sugden line 'I Made Gravy Under Shellfire'. Unfortunately it's not quite true. Although many of my early Army moments were spent in the cookhouse, by the time the shellfire came within my earshot I had graduated to making laughter instead of gravy.

Apart from the Africa Star, all the medals I

wear in Coronation Street are my own, including the Normandy Veterans' badge on my blazer. I might not look old enough because I keep myself fit. When people ask how, I always say: "Jogging. I never do any."

I like Percy very much and although he can be pompous and he is inclined to pontificate I very much admire the respect he shows to other people. He might lodge with Emily Bishop but he would never call her by her first name. Mrs Bishop is Mrs Bishop.

Every time Percy puts his shoulders back he is an old soldier. A lot of people say to me it is easy to recognise you as an old soldier because of your attitude. I am very proud of that. When you went on parade you had to be bright, you had to be smart, and you had to be articulate.

I always had a strong voice. It was developed as an NCO in the Army and then later to carry without the help of microphones to the back of some very big theatres. And I've still got it today. At our Coronation Street Christmas party the cast were all milling around having a chat, when Carolyn Reynolds our executive producer wanted everyone called to order and she said to me: "Go on Bill. Use your Army voice." I barked a couple of 'give order, please' instructions and they all jumped to it. Johnny Briggs said afterwards that he almost jumped out of his skin. You don't lose an edge to your voice like that.

I very much enjoyed the storyline when Percy met up with an old adversary from the German Army. He was played by a smashing chap, an actor who lived in Berlin. One day I happened to mention I liked a smart pair of braces he was wearing and he took them off and gave them to me.

At first old Percy did not at all fancy meeting him, but after we had shared a few drinks we sat in the Rovers singing Lilli Marlene - me in English and him in German. I really enjoyed those scenes. And do you know afterwards the whole studio stood and applauded. I've never heard it at technical run-through before. Afterwards I had a lot of letters about that scene, it really struck a chord with many of our viewers.

I understand why Percy was reluctant to fraternise with the old enemy. I know exactly how Percy feels because it is how I feel as well.

I can forgive but I will never forget.

The Germans were very, very good soldiers but they did some unspeakable things to people along the way. I don't think anyone should forget that. Lessons learned from history are the best lessons of all. The Germans thought they were going to conquer the world. It took the British to stop them.

I believe the way we can confront even the direst adversity with humour is a fantastic national strength. At one time the shortages of rationing did bite extremely hard. There seemed to be queues for everything.

In Liverpool two women joined the back of a long line of anxiously waiting people. After shuffling a few yards forward in half-an-hour one asked the other. "My this is a slow queue, what is it for?" "I think it's The Tales of Hoffman," was the reply. "Oh great!," said the first woman. "My old fellow will eat anything."

Laughter from adversity. If I ever have a slogan then that is it.

But to be serious we really were a great nation then. There was very little crime, with a common enemy it seemed that we all pulled together. The women worked long hours under difficult conditions in munitions factories to support their menfolk who were away fighting. Vandals and joyriders had mercifully yet to be invented. There was more friendship in every walk of life.

I'll never forget my army number. It's T/100783. The T stood for transport and the number was yours for the duration. I've never forgotten it. Find an old soldier and I bet he'll remember his army number.

When Percy Sugden met the pacifist vicar. He sneered at me for being in the catering corps and I flung back at him. "What are you talking about? An army marches on its stomach!" That wasn't in the original script until I suggested it, but it's true. It's a very old saying.

The War made me grow up. You hear people who never went to college say that they have a degree from the 'university of life'. Well five years of soldiering including being part of the Normandy Landings qualifies you for a first class honours in that department.

I was not one of the youngest by any means, I went over in the middle of June just after my 28th birthday. There were lads there of only 17 and 18. A lot of them joined up full of enthusiasm for adventure, others were called up. But no-one who went through that was ever the same. I can never get over how many lost their lives.

# *Joining Up*

Whr a soldier I took with me my banjo-ukulele. I had the notion that somehow I might get the chance to continue my practising and even perhaps one day get the chance to entertain with the instrument. In between fighting the Germans and beating Hitler of course.

We had a family friend called Harold Walden, who was a well-established and successful theatre entertainer. He played the ukulele and always fascinated me with his stories of the stage. He knew of my vague ambitions to make my career in the theatre and had served in an Army concert party in the First World War.

With what turned out to be remarkable foresight Harold had provided me with three basic Army gags which were to be the first steps of following in his path.

I volunteered for the War. I thought if everybody stands back waiting to be called up that's no good. I was very upset about the Germans trampling all over the place. I thought I'd have a go and even with all these years of hindsight I don't think it was the wrong decision. A lot of people stayed out of the Army on some pretext or other and made a lot of money. Personally, I'm glad I went. I can wear medals with pride.

I suppose to be honest I was a bit selfish. I thought if I went in early I would be able to choose what I did a bit more easily. I didn't want to be in the infantry, I preferred the mobile unit because I knew I could always drive. I chose to go in the Royal Army Service Corps, being a volunteer I got that sort of preference.

When I went for my medical in Manchester the doctor looked at my records and said: "You've had rheumatic fever. We can't use you." I was absolutely crestfallen. I felt as fit as a fiddle. As if to make me feel better he added: "I tell you what though, young man. You've got the nicest feet I've seen." Charming I thought. If my feet are as nice as all that why won't you let me march into action with them.

I was very disappointed. But I wasn't going to be kept out of the War that easily. I told my parents there were so many would be recruits there that I came away. Next day I went to Bury barracks and blow me if the doctor there didn't pick me out for rheumatic fever as well. I was getting worried about this. The next day I went over to Bolton barracks and it was the same doctor I had seen the first time. This time he looked at me and said: "My, you're determined." And he gave me a wink and said: "OK you're A1."

It was an enormous relief. But in myself I felt so well I was disappointed than any medical man should ever consider me anything less than A1. I was a very strong young man, physically strong, I could do a one-handed snatch and push on a bar bell of 120 lb. I was very tough. Fellows a lot older would tackle me and finish up on their backs. I was never aggressive but I could hold my own with anyone. I had been taught boxing to help me get over rheumatic fever.

I was healthy and fit and I looked at it this way. 'There is a war coming, they need volunteers and somebody has got to go and fight it. Why not me?' I just thought it had to happen. I told my father I was going to join up. I could see by the look on his face he approved.

"Good lad," he said. He was in the First World War himself, so he had an idea what I was letting myself in for. He said: "I think you are doing the right thing, joining up now. You will have more of a choice of what you want to do if you get in now." This was well before the

> There was a time when the Army decided to copy the Japanese and set up its own kamikaze unit. The Sergeant yelled at us: "Kamikaze volunteers one step forward, MARCH!" Everyone stepped forward except for one man. The Sergeant bellowed:"What is your name?" "Chow mein," came the answer. "First name?" demanded the Sergeant. "Chicken."

call-up for all able-bodied men of the right age came.

When I went off to War my mother came to the station with me to see me off to Aldershot. Her parting words as the train steamed out of the station were: "Goodbye son. Be a good lad and don't fight."

I had to smile. Not that I wanted to fight anyone, I just thought it might be a bit difficult to avoid a scrap in wartime. The concerns over my rheumatic fever disappointed me. But I was very determined. I have never been very good at taking No for an answer when I want to hear Yes and I certainly didn't like it then. I was given the perfect excuse to miss out on the War altogether but that was the last thing I wanted.

In any case I think they must have got it wrong, because here I am at 77 going on 78. At the time I thought if my life is going to be that short I had better use it.

It was just after the occasion when Chamberlain came back from Munich saying Peace in our Time. He reckoned Germany wanted peace. It turned out they wanted a piece of this and a piece of that and a piece of just about everything.

But after 24 hours in the Army at Aldershot I wished I hadn't tried so hard to join up. We were given the most revolting food I had ever seen - a disgusting meat pie served for some stomach churning reason with fish gravy on. I thought blow this, I don't mind fighting but I want feeding as well so I went sick.

I decided to get straight out so I fell back on my medical complaint. I felt a bit guilty about it but I thought well it's on your record so use your rheumatic fever. I went to the MO and told him and he just shook his head. "No, son," he said. "It says here you're A1. That's good enough for me."

So I was stuck. And it was a real shambles at the start. Loads of us had no proper uniforms. Some had grey flannels, a battledress blouse and a bowler hat on. They fitted us up the best way we could, but we looked a real Fred Karno's Army.

Right at the start I made a mistake because I

had been told by an old soldier how to polish my boots. He used to come in our pub and he'd been in the First World War. He showed me how to bone my boots, to rub little circles on the toe cap with polish and then spit and polish and get your tooth brush out and rub it in very hard. That really made my boots shine.

I did this for our first parade for the want of something to do. It was the worst thing I could have done because the sergeant major walked right down through all the rows and then singled me out.

"Do you see these boots," he barked. "I want to see them all like this tomorrow, everybody get your boots done like this. If you don't know how to do it, ask him." Instantly I was the most unpopular feller in the bloody barracks. I was cleaning boots for hundreds of them. Then the very next morning we had an order of the day on the notice board: 'All boots will not be polished. In future they will be dubbined'. They decided that the polish cracked the leather. So it was all done for nothing.

When I first went down to Aldershot I joined the Royal Army Service Corps. I thought I liked driving so I chose that, and when I was posted down from Aldershot to Gillingham in Dorset after a fortnight I joined the 43rd Wessex, a Plymouth unit which was a division of the RASC.

If Gillingham had been anymore exciting it would have qualified as a dump. The biggest growth industry seemed to be total boredom, apart from the local bone factory where they made glue. The factory looked like a long-abandoned ruin. It smelt foul, was overrun by maggots and had huge holes in the walls. So naturally it became my first semi-permanent home in the Army.

This meant slightly less room for the previous occupants, who mainly numbered assorted families of rats and mice, but they didn't seem to mind.

**How would you serve a sheep's head to the sergeants' mess? Cut its mouth open and take all the brains out. What would you do with the brains? Give them to the officers' mess.**

That was a little bit rough. We were sleeping on the floor, one blanket underneath and one on top. That was all we had and it was a freezing cold winter. In a very short time, thanks to my success in the cookhouse, I was promoted. I got a stripe and I was a lance corporal and I was put in charge of the whole billet.

There must have been a hundred men all sleeping on the floor and it was full of rats and mice and all sorts of creatures. I had very little hair then, at 23 I was almost as bald then as I am now. But fellows next to me with good heads of hair found there were mice making nests in their hair at night. There was even a litter of little pink baby mice in one blokes hair. It was the first time in my life that I was glad I had gone bald.

We were supposed to be soldiers but really we were just dressed-up civilians with no real Army experience. We hadn't done any proper drilling and suddenly this prize specimen of a second lieutenant arrived. He had just been given one pip and seemed to be under the impression he was God. We had some very nice officers in the Army but he was not one of them. He just poked around everywhere in our billet trying to find fault, and he couldn't.

All of a sudden he looked at the windows. He said: "Corporal, I shall be back in half an hour, I want to see all these windows properly cleaned." I said: "Are you sure, sir." He said: "Yes. Don't question my orders. Half an hour and I shall be back."

We didn't do anything, we just sat around

for half an hour until he came back. He said:
"Yes, that's better." I said: "Will you do me a
favour sir." He said: "What's that?". I said:
"Will you tap your stick on the window." He
couldn't, because there wasn't a window in the
place. All the glass had been blasted out months
ago. We used to wake up with snow on our
blankets. He coloured up and marched out
feeling, I hope, every bit as big a berk we
thought he looked. I tried to put it in a nice way
and I think that cured him a little bit.

It was all a very strange experience at that
stage, you very rarely knew where you were
going. You were just marched down to the
station and told what train to catch. 'Walls have
ears' was the slogan so the Army operated by
telling people as little as possible. 'Be like Dad
and keep Mum' which got the women upset,
because a lot of the ladies felt they were
working just as hard as the fellows. They were
just indications of the way everyone thought in
those days.

I liked the camaraderie of being in the Army
more than anything. The uniform you accepted
because it was necessary. I've found in my life
that there are people you like and people you
don't like so much. But in the War somehow

**The CO took off all his clothes,
his little bed to lie on.
He thought it rude
to lie there nude
So he put his old school tie on.**

there was a common bond. I liked pretty well all the lads. We all knew why we were there and we got on.

When we went on the firing range I discovered I wasn't a bad shot. I got three bulls and two inners out of five shots. But the next thing that frightened the life out of me was a list on the daily board for the following people to attend further target practice to become snipers.

I was on the list and I was horrified. I didn't want to be a sniper, picking people off from up in a tree. So when we went on the next shoot I said: "I don't know why they've put me here. I didn't hit all that you know. It must be one of those mistakes."

To make sure I did not get to be a sniper, I put a bullet into each of the targets at either side of me so they did well. Everyone was kept on except me. I never wanted to kill anything.

We were asked for volunteers to do some cooking and I put my hand straight up. I come from a farming and butchering family. My mother ran a string of shops so I knew a bit about preparing food. It was winter time and very cold and I knew it would be warm in the cookhouse so, although some of my new comrades thought I was crazy to volunteer, there was a method in my madness.

I started being quite adventurous with the food. One of my specialities was boiled onions. That seemed to go down well so I did it twice in one week and someone complained they were getting too many boiled onions. I suggested he stay away if he didn't like the grub and that didn't go down too well. But within a month I was transferred into the Officers' Mess. They had a chef there but he was no good. I got my proficiency pay for cooking, which was more than he managed and he was supposed to be a proper chef.

I think they could see I had a bit of discipline about me. My mother had trained me that well. The first thing I did was to make sure the place was nippin' clean. Then I started to vary the menu a bit. I did things like puff pastry and graduated to meat and potato pie with decent gravy and proper Lancashire hotpot and word soon got round.

I had got my first stripe pretty quickly and I was anxious to get home and proudly show it to my parents when I was granted my first 48-hour pass. But travelling by train from down in Dorset up to Castleton near Rochdale was easier said than done.

The train stopped every time the air raid sirens sounded. It just used to pull up, switch all the lights out and wait for the all clear. In the end it took so long to get there I just had time to go in, have a meal with my mother and father and get back on the train back again.

We were well looked after in the Army at that time. I think we got better grub than many of the civilians. But, as I was to say in Coronation Street more than 50 years later, 'An army marches on its stomach.' Fighting men needed looking after.

While I was at Gillingham I really started entertaining. I had taken my ukulele banjo with me and every time I had a spare moment I was learning to play it. I amused myself by strumming a few chords and attempting to improve my playing. this seemed to create an impression that way back in 'Civvy Street' I was something of an entertainer.

The only entertaining I'd ever done was a

A German soldier was spotted on the top of the Eiffel Tower. We shouted up to ask him what he was doing. "I'm waiting to see the white flag from Britain," shouted the German. "It's good pay. And a job for life."

few nervous try-outs in a pub my parents ran - the George and Dragon at Castleton near Rochdale. And then I had been so nervous my foot started doing an involuntary tap dance and I forgot the words of the song I was supposed to be singing. I did have a second go a little later and my mother persuaded me to have a small whisky to boost my confidence. But it didn't work. I was still terrified.

I just knew it was in me somewhere if I could get the right start. Right back when I was six years old the Evangelist's Sunday School in Henshaw Street, Oldham was putting on a play called The Mistletoe Bough and my heart lifted when I found out that there was a part for a jester in it.

But it fell again when I found out that they had picked another lad for it. I was very upset. I used to go to watch all the rehearsals from the back of the hall and when it came to the dress rehearsal this lad got stage fright. All of a sudden he couldn't speak a single word. I saw all the grown-ups looking at each other and saying: "What on earth are we going to do now?"

A little voice piped up: "I could do it." At first they wouldn't take me seriously. They couldn't believe that I knew the words, but I went on and on about it so much that they agreed to give me a chance. I stepped forward and did it without any bother at all.

I remember I had to sing: "Eye-tiddley eye-tie, fee fo fum. You called your jester, here I come." I had heard it so often I couldn't forget it, and I got the part. They made me a wig up out of cotton wool to make me look older and I really began to enjoy myself. Every time I jumped round the room in my jester's outfit the wig would start jumping apart all over the place.

That was the first time I ever went on stage. But even then I had a confidence and I liked the experience. I wasn't nervous and I have a quick mind, I always had as a youngster, and now at last I was starting to learn how to use it.

I had never worked professionally as a comedian before the War, but I could always tell a joke. Before the War I had worked selling medical supplies and also selling cars and I had used humour to make many a successful sale. I love making people laugh.

But it was my faithful old uke that really got me started as an entertainer in the Army. I was on parade one day and this Sergeant Major, who had seen me practising my instrument, came striding over and said: "Waddington. That banjo thing. Can you play it?"

"Oh Yes," I said with a show of confidence I did not really feel. He said: "Right you're in the concert on Sunday." I was paralysed with fear. I knew I could play a bit and tell a story but I didn't relish taking on an audience full of tough lads who were hardly in the mood for laughter. In fact I was petrified. I thought they'll tear me apart. But it all worked out well.

It was to be staged in the local cinema, but it felt like the London Palladium to me. They didn't have a film on Sunday so we put a stage show on, I thought I'll make myself look funny then at least I might get one laugh, padded my stomach so I had a fat belly, then pulled my hair up to make it look even worse than it does, and slapped on a big false moustache. I thought if I wasn't that good at least I'd be hard for them to identify afterwards.

**Mary had a little watch
she wore it on her garter
when the boys asked her the time
she knew what they were after**

My mate Dougie Jordan came from Lancashire like me and the other thing we had in common was that his auntie was a lady butcher like my mother and they were good friends. He was helping me to get ready for this show, and he was a bit worried about how frightened I looked.

His remedy was a drink I had never encountered, the strangely named local delicacy 'scrumpy'. Dougie explained it was only rough cider and assured me it would provide just the relaxation I needed. I was tee-total at the time but I was in serious need of assistance so I drank a glass. It was pleasant enough to drink. I said I don't feel any different.

Dougie offered to fetch me another, so I had a second pint of scrumpy. Apparently shortly after this I made my stage debut. I don't remember the details but it seems I was a minor sensation. The major sent for me the following day on the Monday morning. He said:

"Waddington. Congratulations on your wonderful performance last night. It's rather a pity we had the ladies with us of course, but never mind."

I hadn't got a clue what he was on about because I couldn't remember a thing about it. He went on to say that he was looking round for people of 'reasonable intelligence' - he didn't over-emphasise the intelligence - to earmark as officers to go to OCTU, the officers' training course and he had been intending to put my name forward.

But he went on: "After seeing what you did last night I think you would be a lot more use to the Army as an entertainer to keep the morale of the troops up. That is going to be vital." I thanked him very much because I didn't want to be an officer, it was hard enough being a corporal.

That strange start launched me. After that I grew very fond of the sound of laughter from an audience. I found I liked the experience of being up there on stage. When I started doing the concert parties in Gillingham I realised quite quickly the power of humour. You can often get the most amazing things done by making fun of a situation where if you'd just grumbled and complained nothing would have happened.

The officers we had were a real mixed bunch. Some were marvellous blokes and other were jumped up little twerps. It didn't take long to tell between the two. Often it was the ones who came from nowhere who seemed to have the most to brag about, but that's often the way in life.

I did miss out on the chance to go on to be an officer but I don't regret it. I loved entertaining people. As soon as I heard the sound of an audience laughing, I was hooked. I knew becoming an officer would not help me there. The troops might not have taken too kindly to an officer trying to make them laugh. And I loved using humour when the going became rough.

I believe that everyone has a talent. It's just a question of finding it and learning how to use it. Mine was for making people laugh, and once I discovered I could do it, I never really looked back. But everyone has one. The little old lady who sits at home knitting a pair of socks has a talent. I couldn't do it.

I started organising dances in the village for the lads because there was no entertainment for them. I put on dances, concerts and boxing shows. Dougie was put in charge of boxing. He could handle himself. That was more than you could say for his other friend, a corporal who came from Plymouth. He had worked in Plymouth abattoir humping meat. He was a big fellow, square and built like an outside toilet, as wide as he was high. We had had a few kerfuffles, him and I, because he was a boorish ignorant man.

Dougie asked me if I fancied boxing against him. Dougie knew he would never touch me even though he was way out of my weight. I had learned boxing so I said:"OK, put me down." We squared up to each other in this village boxing tournament, a three rounder. He was about three stone heavier but fortunately I was a lot faster than him.

**Oh you're a Corporal are you? Why didn't you get three stripes? Did your knee pads wear out?**

If he'd ever hit me I'd have gone straight into orbit. But I kept moving and clipping him, and by the end I had beaten this poor fellow quite badly. I was very sorry about it afterwards because he couldn't move. He was just like a punch bag and when I saw him the day afterwards his face was a real mess.

Strangely after that we became very great friends. He came to me and he put his arms round me and said: "Well, you did what you had to do and it hurt a bit but not too much, but I'm not tackling you again." We had half a pint of rough cider together and that was the end of it. I got a medal for that victory which I still have to this day.

I much prefer joking to fighting anyway and there was a time when my ability to tell a funny story saved my life. I was on parade ready for embarkation shortly before the fall of Dunkirk.

I was ready and waiting to be drafted overseas but, when the Major saw me in the line-up as he was walking along doing his inspection, he turned to his Sergeant Major and said: "What's Waddington doing with these men?" The Sergeant Major explained that I had been drafted to France. The Major snorted: "He's not, you know. What are we going to do at Christmas time in this dead-and-alive hole without him to amuse us? Send somebody else in his place." So my entertaining abilities saved me from at least one perilous trip up towards the front line. I was extremely lucky.

I put on the Christmas show of course. I used to write all the shows and produce them. I did not know it at the time but it was tremendous training. At Christmas time, as a lot of the lads had now found girlfriends in the village, I got permission from the colonel for the lads to bring them in. And that led to another totally new experience for number T/100783.

## Chapter Three

# *Marry in Haste*

I was one of the lads who had found a girlfriend. I met this attractive young girl in Gillingham. She was a little bit older than me and I took a shine to her as soon as I saw her. Her father was the village police sergeant. I was kept busy putting on all the entertainments for the troops down there, dances and concerts and so on. I got chatting to her and I liked her.

She was called Evelyn Case and I suppose she was the first girl I had ever imagined myself to be in love with. This was wartime remember, and I started thinking I could go over the other side and be dead and I will never have lived, wouldn't have seen life.

I had just about no experience of the opposite sex before I joined up. My mother was always very protective to me when I was working for her as a butcher. Even when I was 18 she would insist if I was going to the pictures that I did not take a girl. She would say: "Look you've got to be up early in the morning to go to market, you haven't time for that sort of thing." I did know one or two nice girls that I was interested in and I had to keep it a secret. So the first time I got away as a soldier I thought, 'Right I can please myself'.

My mother thought I had too much to do to

> After the War my grandson asked me:"Where's
> your bayonet and your rifle?" I said: "They
> wouldn't let me bring that home. I did bring
> my tin hat and my uniform. My hat's in the
> cellar full of nuts and bolts."
> "Where's your uniform," he asked.
> "It's in the airing cupboard next to the tank."
> My grandson couldn't believe it: "Don't tell me
> you've got a tank up there."

get involved in girls and wanted me to make a success of my life without them. When I told my mother and father that I wanted to make Evelyn my wife she said: "Don't you dare bring any girls here, don't you dare."

My father wrote me a letter saying: "Don't tell your mother I have said this, but if you like the girl, carry on. I'm afraid you'll never get anywhere with your mother." My mother wouldn't even let me take her home. I realise now that in a way I married Evelyn totally in defiance of my mother, to be honest. I thought well you can't do anything about it. I'm of age, I'll marry the girl. But she still wouldn't let me take her home, I would have found out a lot more about her if I had. I'm like that, I can be a bit stubborn, if somebody says you're not going to do that I say I will just to show you I can if it kills me.

I don't want to blame my mum but she was responsible in a way for not letting me have experience of girls before I went in the Army. I hadn't got much social experience before the War but at Gillingham I used to arrange all the dances as well as the entertainments and I started to make real grown up friends away from home for the first time. So when someone wanted to be with me and to talk to me I was very flattered. Evelyn was quite an attractive woman, a little bit older than me, and she seemed a nice person.

She paid me some attention, and it was a natural thing, the attraction between us. I never touched her before we got married, never at all, because I was not that way. I wasn't looking for women other than for good friendship, somebody to dance with and somebody to be with a bit different from the young lads I was soldiering with. I was 24 when I got married. I suppose if I'd had experience before then I don't think I would have fallen in love quite as easily as I did. I did it out of defiance.

So I married her. If I'd had the guts, I would have turned round and walked out on the day of the wedding. Because, at almost the last minute, I had received a message from the hotel where my sister and her husband were staying in Gillingham. The landlord had been talking to them saying that I shouldn't go ahead with this marriage because they had found out a lot of things about Evelyn that I did not know.

But it was too late then, because that was only a few days before. I did not want to go back on my word but I was even wavering the night before. The landlord said that she had had a lot of boyfriends, that she was 'the pride of the village' and particularly insisted that she had been carrying on with the local postman.

When they told me about my bride-to-be I dismissed it as all idle gossip. The truth was that I simply didn't want to hear it. But somehow all emotions were heightened in wartime. In my mind, I was always thinking 'I could get sent off to fight and be killed and I will never have lived.'

Almost straight away after the wedding I knew it was all a horrible mistake. We were a married couple but I was still in the Army so we were living separately. I was young and very inexperienced in life and I was daft. Having a girl who was attractive and fun to dance with and lark around with was quite different from having a woman to share your

> A fly landed on my plate one day
> so poorly in half dead fashion
> it looked dead beat
> without no meat
> so I gave him half my ration

whole life with. But then I was moved away, to Hertford which was an enormous relief. My suspicions about the other men in her life had long been confirmed so there was no feeling for Evelyn left in me.

It was painful but that didn't stop it giving rise to yet another gag. Humour comes from all shades of life. At least that must have been how I felt when I came up with this one.

A young fellow meets a beautiful girl in the village and they got on very well and he started thinking: "I'm a young man. It's wartime. I could go off and get killed and never have slept with a woman."

So they decided to get married. They went to see the local vicar and said they wanted to wed. Right away. He told them: "Oh, you can't get married straight away. We have to post the banns of marriage for three consecutive Sundays."

The couple's faces fell. Suddenly the lad had

# Chapter Three

an idea. He piped up: "Couldn't you just say a few words to tide us over the weekend."

I'm afraid I was very deceitful where Evelyn was concerned, I just wanted to put her right out of my mind, so I pretended I could never get back to Gillingham.

I did go back once more on a Christmas leave but I got a soldier pal called Clifford Davis - the same chap who was on the Daily Mirror in Fleet Street and much later the Mr Nasty on the panel in New Faces - to send me a telegram pretending I had to report back to my unit immediately. So I did not even stay another night with Evelyn. I was so relieved to get away and in fact I was wanted, to organise a special show for Christmas.

I'm not particularly proud of it but after that I just never went back. I realised by then that what everyone had told me before was right. There was no feeling left between us and after that I just put her right out of my mind. It was not until after the War, when I met a beautiful leading lady called Lilian Day, that I realised I had to tidy up that area of my life. Lilian was the love of my life and I very much wanted to marry her.

I met Lilian when we were working

together in my first pantomime after the War. She was a very beautiful principal boy and I was a very silly Wishee Washee. I noticed straight away what an attractive woman she was but I did not imagine she would look twice at a joker like me.

The day we met, I was doing a night-time broadcast in London. I was already working at the Empire, Croydon down in south London, coming in to the West End to rehearse pantomime and getting time out to go and rehearse a broadcast. I was all over the place. I even had to rush off in a taxi between houses to do a radio broadcast at Marble Arch.

Straight away I thought Lilian was a nice person. But I also thought she was bound to have a husband, a smart girl like that. But she was like me she was very choosy. But I never imagined she would be interested in a bald-headed comic like me. The only thing going for me really was that I could make her laugh. She had a very good sense of humour and that became one of the strong bonds between us.

I think that week I earned £85 which was an awful lot of money in those days. I got back to Swindon and got paid on the Saturday night and I couldn't get to the bank and I wrapped

> A young officer on parade says:
> "Everybody. Left knee, raise." one
> soldier raised his right leg instead.
> The officer looked slowly down the line
> and asked: "Right. Who is the silly ass
> with two legs in the air?"

my money in a handkerchief and left it in my pocket in my dressing room. When we rehearsed on Sunday I found just an empty handkerchief and someone had stolen all my money. I had worked all that bloody week for nothing. But in my heart I knew I was well in profit because I had met Lilian.

But I was still trapped in this unhappy marriage, I wanted very much to get out of it. I had no interest in seeing or hearing from my wife again. Lilian was staying in digs and I was in an hotel not very far away. I offered to walk her down, just nice, I was never one of these blokes who are very forward with women. The panto went on for about six weeks and her mother came down to see the pantomime. They were going off down to Folkestone and I carried her bags to the station for her which went down well with her mother.

She said, 'What a nice young man!' They

weren't used to be being looked after like that. And our relationship built up very quietly from that. We went down to Folkestone and we happened to be staying in the same digs this time. She had her room and I had my room and we had our meals together and we gradually got to know each other a bit better. I remember we were having a meal one night and the landlord came in and said: "My daughter is having a baby in the next room so don't be alarmed if you hear some screaming or unusual noises." We felt sorry for this poor girl in the only room they had available for her, Lilian never forgot it and in a funny way it brought us closer together.

Of course, technically, I was still married, but Lilian started touring the country with me. By then I desperately wanted a divorce. Evelyn was long since out of my life but I needed to make it official. In the end Evelyn would not budge so Lilian and I gave her grounds, and that was the end of the road.

It was a wartime romance, one of millions that never worked out. Only in my case there was a bitter little postscript. Long after I had last been back Evelyn had a baby, a boy. I knew there was no way I could have been the lad's father.

But she said that her son was my child and rather than argue with her I paid maintenance for him until he was 16 just in case he was. In those days it was peanuts, but I never thought he was my son. People who knew us both told me that he did not resemble me in any shape or form. Not in a million years was he my son.

As soon as I got my divorce through, she married this postman. Then I found out that, although I was paying maintenance for this boy Spencer, they had changed his name to that of the postman. So he is not known as Spencer Waddington. He wrote to me once and said he thought he was my son. I wrote back and said: 'I don't have a son with a name like that.' He wrote and asked if I wanted to meet my grandchildren. I said: 'I don't think they are my grandchildren. I haven't got any'. He asked if he could met me on the quiet. I said: 'I don't want to meet you on the quiet. If you're my son and you can prove it, I will be very pleased to meet you - but I don't think you are, because you've got your father's name.' So that was the end of it.

If I had really felt he was my son, I would have been proud to have him. But I don't believe he is. These sort of things happen in wartime.

# *The Blue Pencils*

In view of my unhappy marriage I was delighted when our unit was ordered, in the autumn of 1940, to move to Hertfordshire. Officially I was still in charge of the cookhouse but I was doing more and more entertaining by then and my confidence was really starting to grow.

They asked me to do a spot in a big show on a Sunday night at the local cinema in Hertford. I had a little more idea about what I was doing by then and I most certainly wasn't drunk. As well as troops, there were civilians in the audience. I was decked out in what had become my stage outfit - small tin hat, whitened face, large false moustache, old-fashioned striped bathing costume and ukulele.

**Was that thunder or bombs? Bombs. Thank goodness. I thought we were going to have some more rain.**

I reasoned that if I looked funny then perhaps that would help me to be funny. And that particular evening it appeared to pay off. It was one of those marvellous nights when everything went just right and even if I do say it myself, I paralysed them.

The following morning I left the camp to go into the centre of Hertford to have trimmed

> We went to the fairground one night and
> we were shooting at ping pong balls
> bouncing on spouts of water. I had one
> shot and they all went down. How did you
> do that asked the Sergeant Major. I shot
> the woman working the pump.

what little hair I still had left. The barber saw
from my uniform that I was with the Royal
Army Service Corps unit that had just arrived
and asked me if I had seen last night's show.
Out of that bizarre get-up he didn't recognise
me. I couldn't resist running through some of
my act to convince him he was snipping away
at the very man who had amused him.

That's when a flash of luck came in to
change my life. By chance the newly formed
Blue Pencils concert party had also arrived in
Hertfordshire that day to do a series of shows
for the troops in aid of the Army Benevolent
Fund.

And just a little later that Monday morning
the Captain in charge, an experienced theatre
producer by the name of T.Y. Benyon, himself
went in to that same Hertford barber's to have
his hair cut. Just making conversation, as they
do, the barber asked the Captain what he was
doing in that part of the world.

This was at the frightened time of 'Careless Talk Costs Lives' yet it has occurred to me many times since that day that, had Hitler recruited Britain's barbers as information gatherers, then far more of our secrets would have found their way to the Germans. Barbers would have been wonderful secret agents.

Captain Benyon explained that he was there with a team of entertainers, engaged in the important business of raising morale and very much on the lookout for any new talent among the troops. The barber perked up: "You should have been here last night. We had a comic on who was absolutely hilarious." He went on to tell this sitting-target of a Captain some of my more memorable jokes. "If you want a good comic you want to go and get Bill Waddington, he's a scream."

And, to my eternal gratitude, that's exactly what he did. I got my big chance as part of The Blue Pencils Concert Party. They had a comic in the show already but he was a West End type who was stylish and sophisticated enough, but rubbish as far as the lads were concerned. I had a head start in being in tune with the troops. After all I was already one of them.

I was called in for an audition and I went up

before Captain Benyon and his assistant, one Sergeant Phillip Merrick, a singer of some note who had appeared in the 1938 Royal Command Performance with Evelyn Laye. He was a well known light opera and musical comedy tenor whose career had been interrupted by hostilities. But there were just the two of them, looking serious and businesslike, hardly the most promising audience to greet a nervous comedian just after breakfast in an empty theatre.

When I arrived up there on the stage by myself Captain Benyon just said: "Right, make us laugh." It was quite a challenge but I managed it, even at nine o'clock in the morning.

Fortunately I am blessed with a quick wit and a gift of the gab that has never deserted me. I thought: 'this is terrible, talking to a lot of chairs,' and I took these two into my confidence. I pretended that any minute someone else would be coming in, and that I wanted to tell them all about me before anyone else arrived.

At one point, presumably to test whether I really could think on my feet, Phil Merrick asked: "Waddington, if you saw ten heavily-armed Germans coming towards you, what would you do?"

"Well sir," I said, "if I had feet as big as yours, I'd drop down into my boots and fire at them through my laceholes." And I managed to get this pair laughing with nonsense like that. Afterwards Captain Benyon

They asked me what I did in Civvy Street. Rather optimistically I answered, 'I'm a comedian.' 'Oh you'll be at home here,' came the reply. 'The sergeant's mess is full of them.'

laughed and applauded and went off almost immediately to ask the War Office if he could have me in his concert party. Thankfully he got the go ahead and that was a very important turning point for me. He got the vital permission and I went into the show as a principal comic.

It opened up a totally new world to me. I was still a soldier of course, but it dawned on me that I was also an entertainer. My ability as a driver was quickly recognised and I frequently found myself behind the wheel of our touring bus. We were a tight little team and it was all very well organised. We even had an advance manager called Inky Ingram who went round and found billets for all of us.

Usually people were very kind and happily put us up. We stayed with some very nice folk. I remember a doctor and his family who gave me lodgings near Cambridge. They had two very bright young sons. This was at a time when all the signposts had been taken down in case the Germans invaded. I was chatting to his father about this when this little six-year-old piped into our conversation. He suggested they went a little further with the confusion and swopped all the signposts round. Then as he put it, in a remark that has always tickled me: "At least then you would know you were somewhere you weren't."

I think the only time we didn't get a warm welcome was when this snooty woman refused Inky's request for accommodation and snorted: "I'm not having scruffy soldiers staying in my house." She was bombed three days later.

Soon afterwards we arrived in a place called Baldock for a show at the local town hall. While we were there the BBC came along from London and said they would like to broadcast the show. I was completely knocked out. Me, Bill Waddington, former car salesman and butcher's boy, on the radio. I pinched myself to

**The vicar announces hymn number 149 'Art thou weary? Art thou languid?' I got seven days CB (confined to barracks) for saying Yes.**

make sure I wasn't dreaming.

It was an important moment for me when I wrote home and said I was doing my very first radio broadcast from Baldock in Hertfordshire. I realised as we went on the radio, that although I was doing an act I'd been doing for a little bit of time, my mother and father had never seen me perform properly, only witnessed a few nervous ramblings in a crowded pub that added up to the best part of not very much.

I knew that night, as the radio beamed our show across the nation, that back at home in the pub listening were my mother and father. My poor dad was more nervous than I was - he went upstairs, he couldn't bear to listen. He said to my mother: "Oh no! I can't stand it, he'll make a mistake." He had only seen me amateurishly try to amuse a few customers in the pub without any noticeable success. He didn't know I'd learned a bit since then.

As it turned out that first radio chance went very well. The pub was full of laughter and halfway through the programme my mother shouted upstairs: "Come down Will. He's marvellous!"

Later, when I went home, I realised that my mother was so proud of me. And she said that on the night of that first broadcast my father took a bottle of Dimple Haig whisky, which was not easy to come by, off the bar shelf and announced: "I won't touch that until my lad comes home out the Army." And he kept to his word.

Soon afterwards, on Christmas Eve in 1940 I got a write-up in the *Daily Mail* that meant a lot. The story was headed 'Army Comedian Is On His Way To Fame'. I've had a lot of publicity in the 50-odd years since then, but I've never had an article that meant more to me.

That faded cutting is in my aged scrapbook but I can still recall every word without reference to it. It said:

*Lance-Bombardier William - Bill to us - Waddington drives 'The Blue Pencils' (the 40th A.A. Brigade Mobile Concert Party) round 500 square miles of England in their own bus to give a concert every night.*

*He is also their leading comedian. And a very good comedian, too. You are going to hear more of Bill Waddington after the War.*

*He is a 24-year-old Manchester butcher, but if he is wise he will forsake the joint for the jest, because he is a natural comedian, a flour-faced* comedian, with a slow stolid, unsmiling style of comedy.

Two months ago he had no more idea than you or I that he would be making a large audience laugh every night and three afternoons a week (free matinees for the troops).

But after a breakfast time audition with Captain T.Y. Benyon, Bill Waddington was recruited as a valuable  new member of The Blue Pencils.

Captain Benyon said, 'If you can make me laugh at nine o'clock in the morning, you'll do.' He did. And he has been bringing the house down ever since.

Like George Formby, he wears immaculate evening dress, but he adds a tin helmet as a touch of his own. Like George Formby, too, he plays a ukulele and sings in the broadest Lancashire.

But, unlike George Formby, he never smiles, and his technique is entirely different. He wants it to be. The last thing he wants is to be just another Formby.

He writes his own songs and patter, and his signature gag is 'Listen, missus,' which always goes over as well as Max Miller's 'Nark it!'

You may hear 'The Blue Pencils' on the air in mid-January. If so, listen for two more names,

*Bombardier Cyril Haberman and Gunner Ronnie Keylock.*

*Bombardier Haberman, in peace-time a member of the London Stock Exchange, is a ventriloquist with a neat line in patter and (except when he is talking artfully between his teeth on the dummy's behalf) has a great booming voice that hits the rafters and comes bouncing back. Refreshing indeed in these days of microphone mania.*

*Gunner Keylock, formerly an underground electrician, is only 20, a self-taught accordionist who used to play in London's champion accordion band.*

*'The Blue Pencils' are 17 strong, nine men (all soldiers turned full-time entertainers) and eight girl volunteers. They play in theatres, town halls, church halls - anywhere in the brigade area where there are troops. The men sleep in the halls and in barracks.*

When I read that I felt about 10 feet tall. That gave me a great kick, because I was clean, I was fresh and I was funny and I was doing jokes about things of the moment. I wrote my own material and, wonderfully, it worked.

The Press went round to my mother and father's pub to do a 'local boy makes good' story. I winced a bit when I heard that one of the first things my father did was to get out this old school report of mine where the headmaster had written: "Your son is clown for the class."

I have to admit it was true, at school I was always prepared to do anything for a little bit of fun. It wasn't a case of being maliciously naughty. It was just good, old-fashioned fun as far as I was concerned.

The Northern Edition of *Thompson's Weekly News* reported:

> *Years ago a rather perturbed father hurried round to ask why the local headmaster had called his son the 'Clown for the class' in his end of term report.*
>
> *He was told that the lad just couldn't resist joking even at the expense of his studies.*
>
> *This week the father and mother listened to the forces wireless programme, heard their son, now a 24-year-old soldier, smash-hit the ether in his radio debut as a Lancashire comedian.*
>
> *He's Lancashire all right, born and brought up in Oldham, and his friends there know he is a comedian. But it took the War and his Army*

commanding officer to show him he could put it
across the footlights - and the wireless waves.

Note the name - Lance-Bombardier Bill
Waddington. You'll probably be hearing lots more
of this white-faced, unsmiling figure in a rather
weird full evening dress topped by a tin hat.

His parents, Mr and Mrs Waddington, live at
the Queen Ann Inn, Shaw, near Oldham. When
Mrs Waddington used to carry on a butcher's
business in Oldham, Bill, the only son, delivered
the meat. Customers listened for his coming
because they knew him as the whistling butcher's
boy.

He belonged to the parish church choir but
never had any concert experience until he
enlisted.

"Bill joined the RASC," his father said, "and
it was his commanding officer who discovered
him. Soon Bill was in such great demand he could
hardly manage to entertain all those who wanted
him.

"He began to appear regularly with the Blue
Pencils concert party and he hopes after the War
to make a stage career. He has already received a
good offer if he could have been released from
service, but this was not possible.

"When Bill joined up he told me he would

*just take his ukulele along in case it might come in handy. Now it is inseparable from his act. He writes his own songs and composes the tunes as well.*

*"Home on leave a few days ago he sang us his latest number, which he has not made public yet. It's so catchy I'm sure it will prove popular." Mrs Waddington commented: "It was a bit frightening hearing Bill over the radio. I kept wondering would he make a mistake. I shouldn't have worried though for he enjoys doing his act even more than his audience like listening to it.*

*"His broadcast was actually the first time I or my husband had ever heard him give his performance in public."*

It's a fantastic feeling finding that there is something that you can do. I knew when I heard people laughing at what I was saying that I liked the experience. Now I realised that one day I really might be able to 'forsake the joint for the jest'. Even though it had really been my mother who had been the butcher. I'd worked in her shops before the War. But I knew then that I wasn't going back.

Brigadier Nicholson, a member of the famous Gin family, was the officer in charge of the Blue Pencils, and fortunately I appealed to his sense of humour. He came to see me afterwards beaming all over his face and said: "That was absolutely marvellous, Waddington. Just the job to cheer up the men."

He used to come every three weeks to make sure the show was up to par. He always sat on the front row. I would look out for him and make sure I had a new gag or two ready so he didn't think he had heard it all before.

The Blue Pencils were my passport to the start of a long career in broadcasting. At that time the BBC had a series of radio programmes called Ack-Ack, Beer-Beer produced by a wonderful man called Bill McLurg.

I felt very privileged because he didn't ask me to audition he just gave me a time and asked me to come on after watching my act. And during the War I did more programmes than any other comedian - I am very proud of that record.

We had so many laughs touring round the country. In one seaside town I picked up the local paper and read on the front page all about the marriage of Mr Alcock and Miss Addit. You couldn't make up names like that. I had it framed and put on the wall and I've always remembered them. I never forget anything that has fun in it.

Of course there was a serious message behind The Blue Pencils, which had been first launched in May 1940. It was well summed up in the programme notes written by Captain Benyon for a show at the Arts Theatre, Cambridge in December 1941.

The language seems strangely formal after all these years but I think he summed up the aims of The Blue Pencils rather well.

> *The Concert Party was formed with the object of providing additional entertainment for Troops scattered over the countryside where there was not a great deal of alternative entertainment.*
>
> *Then came the question of finance and it was felt that the Party could serve a dual purpose in also playing to members of the public, thereby paying expenses and, furthermore, any profits accruing could be devoted to a Welfare Fund.*
>
> *The second object was one of necessity. When permission to form the Party was given by the Army authorities it was laid down that no charge on public funds would be allowed.*
>
> *One officer and ten men were allocated from Army personnel but there was a feeling that some*

feminine element would be appreciated, and, accordingly, certain ladies were selected from a large number who responded to an appeal and voluntarily gave of their services. There were no donations, subscriptions or gifts available and the Party was launched on credit and with overpowering liabilities.

The attainment of the object was soon quite evident and all expenses in connection with the Party - transport, costumes, scenery etc are provided out of the proceeds of public performances. Electric lighting and painting of scenery are carried out by members of the Party.

The proceeds, after payment of expenses, are allocated to the 2nd AA Divisional Welfare Fund, inaugurated and under the direction of Mrs F.M. Grove-White.

The fund exists for aiding cases of exceptional hardship among wives, families and dependents of serving troops. This aid covers a wide range and has met a heavy demand where wives and families have suffered through  bombing.

The fact that the Concert Party has filled a great need in both objects is instanced by the following details. Since the launching of the Party in May 1940:The number of troops and Public entertained: 73,000

*Performances given: 245*
*Donations to the Welfare Fund have reached a considerable sum, and it is hoped before long to pass into four figures."*

I was very proud to be asked to join The Blue Pencils and delighted to have been able to continue raising money for such a good cause from that day to this. The Army Benevolent Fund, as it is known today, will always be the charity closest to my heart. If I go out on an after-dinner speaking engagement or present a prize to a big bingo winner I find it hard to do without first negotiating a cheque for the Army Benevolent Fund.

And by the way I should say thank-you to you, the reader, for helping. My profits from the sales of this book will go to the Army Benevolent Fund because I know what wonderful work the charity does in helping deserving old soldiers and their families.

That programme also contains a wonderfully nostalgic note about the possibility of air raids:

*"If an air raid warning be received during the performance the audience will be informed from the stage.*

*The warning will not necessarily mean that a raid will take place and in any case it is not likely to occur for at least five minutes. Those desiring to leave the theatre may do so, but the performance will continue."*

It is those last four words that amuse me today: "The performance will continue." A little thing like a few tons of explosives hurled out of the sky was not going to affect the important work of the Blue Pencils. How I still admire that attitude.

The Arts Theatre was a marvellous place for our show, a musical revue called *Go To It*. We were on the same stage where Alec Guinness had starred in *Thunder Rock* and Alastair Sim had appeared in *Cottage To Let* just a few weeks before.

Every now and then I had to pinch myself. I was in showbusiness.

Touring the country in a creaking old bus was fabulous fun. We didn't have an Army lorry because were not supposed to be taking anything from the War effort. And often I would be behind the wheel. We went all over the country in our mission to entertain.

At the Royal Hall, Harrogate, where I was

doing a Just William routine as well as playing Idle Jack in our potty panto, I almost lost my voice. I got treatment for my throat in the wonderful local spa baths and they got me right which was a great relief.

In those days there was no using microphones to make yourself heard in the back row. You had to project. I had a strong voice and I was pleased to get it back. Even in big theatres that could hold 2,000 people I could always make myself heard. I still can.

One of the big stars of the day was Wee Georgie Wood and I was highly delighted when I was given a handwritten note, dated February 2nd, 1942, in which he said:

*"Please let me say how much I enjoyed the originality of your programme on Ack-Ack, Beer-Beer today. I don't wonder you're nearing your 500th performance. You showed how unnecessary studio audiences are. Thank-you and good luck!*

I did get to meet him years later in South Wales when I topped the bill over him in Swansea. He wasn't so pleased then. It really upset him, I'm afraid.

After the Blue Pencils was such a success, lots of copycat organisations came along like the Norfolk Turkeys, Thumbs Up and The

> It was Christmas Day in the Army.
> The soldiers were all underfed.
> They had no Christmas pudding,
> because the Sergeant had done what they said.

Mustard Pots. But I was frequently called in to appear as a guest comic with these other troupes because, to put it frankly, the comedians they had were too crude.

I was never rude, I've never liked blue material and I've never done it. So I became stand-by comedian for all these other outfits - that's why I came to do so many broadcasts. That in itself was a compliment to me. If I could be funny enough to get away with entertaining without being filthy, then that is the only way I would ever want to do it.

They were marvellous times with the Blue Pencils. Everything changed for me when I joined the Army's first concert party. It was such a wonderful door opening for me to do this entertainment business. Because I was working with people I could stand up with. They were talented but they weren't fantastic pros because all the great big names were kept out of the War to entertain on a larger scale. So I had the chance to have a go without being overshadowed.

For me it worked because I was lucky enough to take to broadcasting and I was quick enough to write my own material. I was often billed the Army's number one comic and it was a title I was always determined to live up to. I always tried to find something new.

We went all round the country, particularly in the east of England. I have many happy memories of Norfolk. We had a very good team and we used to take all our own scenery. Ronnie Keylock was a brilliant electrician, he would tap us into the main electricity supply. Sometimes he switched so much power to the hall we were playing in, that he would black the village out. So the audience had to come to see the show to get a bit of light!

I remember that incident very clearly because I was billeted in a lovely old cottage and the lady of the house was very attentive indeed. She was about thirty-five. I've no idea where her husband was, or even if she had one. She cooked me some lovely grub and in those days of rationing that was most welcome. But her next move really startled me.

It was towards the end of the week, I had

just finished my supper she asked if I had enjoyed the meal and then she said: "If you would like something else you know where my bedroom is."

I was speechless! I didn't go up to my bedroom right away, but sat wondering if I had really heard her correctly. Then I went up and lay on my bed wondering if I should chance it. I thought: "Well, it's wartime. I could be dead next week and I've never lived." Finally, without too much difficulty and heart-searching, I managed to talk myself into making the effort.

All the curtains were pulled back in the darkness even though we had blackout regulations to conform to. There I was, in my pyjamas, with the moonlight glinting off my bald head, creeping carefully into my lady's chamber.

She was fast asleep and I leant forward to tap her affectionately on the shoulder. Her eyes opened, and she saw me in the moonlight, and she let out a scream that must have woken half the village. I realised then that I had misunderstood. "Something else," was never mentioned again.

The girls were very talented. Often they

An officer in the First World War says to his men in the trenches. "Right men when I blow this whistle I want you to jump up there as one man and rush into the attack. Over the top and the best of luck."He blows his whistle and they all jump out and rush off, except for one man who jumps back. "What are you doing soldiers? Didn't you hear my orders?" bellows the officer. "I'm not going up there," said the soldier. "They've gone mad. They are killing one another."

were from big West End shows and even after the War I've kept in touch with them. To this day The Blue Pencils have annual reunions but I've attended only once. Working on Coronation Street has meant I've had to miss out.

Clifford Davis, who was a member of the Blue Pencils and a journalist, was quite a pal of mine at first. He came to write and to compere on our tours.

I got on quite well with him until one day I found out that he had had a book published by French's of comedy sketches and he was using stuff of mine without permission. I went mad. I was going to kill him and he was a much bigger fellow than me. I told him: "If you ever do anything like that again I'll take my chances with you." I wouldn't have pinched any of his stuff, not that any of it was worth pinching. I had a right go at him.

He was a pompous person and I think he was very jealous of me. The officer in charge took me to the back of the hall when Clifford Davis was compere and asked me what I thought. I said: "He's stopping the show and I don't mean with entertainment. He slows it up too much."

The moment he came out on stage, people hated him. I said: 'he's spoiling the show.' And he was taken off. Naturally Clifford was not best pleased when he found out the nature of my advice. And he was the worst conjuror I've ever seen.

After the War he came up to Blackpool when I was doing my first summer season. He got in touch and said he was doing an article about all the comics in the resort. But when it came out, I was played right down and he raved about other comics who are long since forgotten. I know I was trying to get his own back, but I didn't care. I went on to do the Royal Command Performance while his tips for the future faded into obscurity.

**I reported sick to the MO once and he asked: "Are you constipated?" "No, I'm Church of England."**

But most of my memories of The Blue Pencils are fond ones. Even when I was admitted to a hospital just outside Birmingham with a very bad back in the summer of 1942, it turned out to be a fascinating experience.

For some reason I was put in a hospital full of Canadian soldiers. I had the distinction of being the only English patient in the place. To keep us busy we were given all sorts of things to do as therapy and I chose to make a small woollen mat.

Lying back working away at my little mat we got the exciting news that the Duke of Kent, who was the youngest brother of King George VI, was to visit the hospital the following week. I'm not sure where I got the idea from but I decided to stitch a piece of canvas to the back of my mat in the hope of getting His Royal Highness to stop by my bed and autograph it for me.

As the Duke toured the wards he was told that the hospital had just the one English patient, so I suppose it was natural enough that he should pick me out to visit. Towards the end of our short conversation I cheekily asked him if he would be kind enough to sign the back of my little mat and he happily agreed.

As soon as the Duke and his entourage had moved on my bed was surrounded by Canadian soldiers offering to buy my keepsake. They almost came to blows in their irritation that none of them had had the foresight - or cheek - to ask their Royal visitor for his signature. They were desperate to own what had suddenly changed from a humble, hand-made therapeutic aid into a highly-prized possession.

But they wouldn't leave it at just asking. They pestered the life out of me so much afterwards. I even got the nurses to hitch my mattress up so I could sleep on it for fear of having it pinched in the night. In the end I decided to raffle the mat. I sold tickets and made a few bob, in fact £28 as I recall, but my mat is now in some old soldier's collection of war memories over in Canada. I'd love to know exactly where it is today.

Its value shot up swiftly soon afterwards because only a few weeks later the Duke of Kent tragically lost his life in an air crash. On August 25 he was killed when a flying boat crashed during a trip to Iceland. It could very well have been his last autograph.

After five weeks my painful back was better

**Jack and Jill went up the hill
just like two cock linnets
Jill came down with half a crown
they hadn't been up two minutes.**

and I was ready to rejoin The Blue Pencils. But I had reckoned without Army bureaucracy. The system said that when you were discharged from hospital you were sent back to Aldershot to be re-assigned to a unit.

I could see my Army entertainment career ending just as soon as it had started so I anxiously tried to persuade the officer in charge that I was a member of a particular Army concert party which was expecting my early return. He would not budge, telling me firmly: "You go to Aldershot and then you get re-posted somewhere else!"

That was all I could get out of him. No matter how much I tried to persuade and explain the situation it made no difference to him. There was only one thing left to do. I walked out of the hospital and got to a public telephone box as quickly as I could. I telephoned Brigade headquarters and managed to get myself put through to Brigadier-General Nicholson.

"What's the trouble, Waddington?" he asked. And I explained that, having got my back better, I faced being prevented from rejoining his concert party. He was marvellous. He just said: "Don't move from the telephone box. Stay where you are and I'll send a staff car for you." He was as good as his word and I travelled back to The Blue Pencils in style. It was comforting to feel that at least the man in charge valued my services.

Brigadier-General Nicholson seemed to take a bit of a shine to me. He said to me: "When this War is over you are going to be a big name. If you need any help, any money to put a show on do not be frightened of asking." I never did, because fortunately I never needed to. I managed it under my own steam. He was a smashing bloke, he always behaved the same to everyone regardless of rank.

He was a real gentleman from the old school. Later, when he got his bowler hat - as they call retirement from the Army - he gave us a wonderful party. And he asked us if there were any secrets we had kept from him. Over a lavish duck supper I confessed to him about the time I had briefly reached his rank.

It was in Wolverhampton, of all places,

**This Sergeant Major we had thought a lot of himself. Someone asked him what he did in Civvy Street. He said he was in the timber business. And he was. I saw him myself after the War. Outside a theatre selling matches.**

where we did a sketch in which I played a Brigadier General. We were so short of uniforms that my own best uniform was used as my costume, adorned with the red tabs, the crown and swords, and the rest of the insignia. As we were going on leave the next day I asked the officer in charge if I could get another uniform as my usual outfit was filthy due to shifting scenery. He was too busy to help and just brushed me off.

The only thing I could do was to take my dirty uniform to the dry cleaner's in Wolverhampton. And the only uniform I had to wear in the meantime was the Brigadier General's.

I took the risk and wandered around the town all morning receiving courteous salutes from a host of soldiers. My friend, Sergeant Frank Myers, was with me, and was petrified throughout. I must have looked the youngest Brigadier General in the British Army by a mile.

The lads used to love that routine when I

dressed myself up as this twit of an officer called De Vere Farquharson-Farquharson Bart: "I want to talk to you today about current affairs. Is there anyone here who has had an affair with a current?

"This lecture has been compiled by Professor Campanini. Do you remember his brother Professor Camping-out-y, the inventor of the Nissen hut? It is an alphabetical description of Who's Who at the Zoo. Under letter A we have the alligator which does not wear a garter, but then neither does a camel wear a camisole..."

I said to our Sergeant Major, 'I pray for you every night.' He said, 'Do you? Why, thank you very much.' I said, 'No, don't thank me. You're still here.'

I used to call for questions from the audience of troops and I used to have a bloke planted. He would put his hand up and ask me: "What is the biggest race in the world?" "The Derby," I suggested. "No, sir." "The Grand National." "No, sir." "All right you tell me." "The human race," he would say as he started laughing. "I don't know what you're laughing at, you don't belong to it."

There were so many marvellous moments

*Fifty years on, the beach at Arromanches was quiet and deserted, but still full of memories.*

*Arromanches seems such a peaceful seaside village today.*

*The British Cemetery at Bayeux. A final resting place for so many brave young lads.*

My first stripe came
after success in the
cookhouse - Percy
would have
approved.

My father served
in World War One. I
think he was proud
when I joined up early.

An early stage outfit was evening dress topped with a tin hat. No wonder they laughed.

I started dressing up very early. This is me as a young Scarlet Pimpernel.

*Arthur Ferrier's cartoon really put me on the map.*
*Even if I didn't like being linked to George Formby.*

*Travelling with Blue Pencils was an amazing introduction to showbusiness.*
*That's me perched on top of our old bus outside the Arts Theatre, Cambridge*

*The concert party in full costume. In my case it was a rather hot knitted swimsuit and it wasn't easy to walk with the crutch of the outfit around my knees.*

*Blue Pencils' leader Captain Benyon has us lining up for our pay. I think I looked sad because I was on the wrong end of the queue.*

Above: Entertaining in newly liberated France was an amazing experience. We tried to mount an invasion of laughter.

Left: As the War drew to a close my new career in Civvy Street included some moments as a recording star. I could hold a tune but laughter was my business.

*It was just after the War when I met the love of my life, Lilian Day. Marrying Lilian was the best move I ever made and even though she sadly died in 1980, I still look at her photograph first thing every morning.*

with the Blue Pencils. I will always remember playing in my first big theatre, the Arts Theatre, Cambridge. I got tremendous publicity and we were honoured by a visit from the famous theatrical cartoonist Arthur Ferrier, whose cartoons of the big West End shows were carried in the News of the World.

He did one of us which was very flattering, except that next to the sketch he wrote: "Bombardier Bill Waddington on his best Formby."

This saddened me because, although I admired George Formby very much indeed, I did not want to look as though I was copying him just because I came from Lancashire and played the ukulele. I stopped playing the uke for quite a time after that. I wanted to be me and nobody else.

The Army was full of humour if you knew where to look. I wrote a routine about getting promotion which always went down well with the lads. When I was a lance corporal it went like this:

"How did you get your stripe?"

"Well, as a matter of fact, it was done when I was medically examined. There were two medical officers present at the examination and they each looked into my ears on opposite sides of me at the same time. And because they could see each other they gave me a stripe!"

Then when I was promoted to corporal, the gag grew.

"I see you've got another one."

"Well, I would have had three only my knee pads ran out."

After a while The Blue Pencils' success was so widely copied and concert parties began springing up all over the place that the army authorities thought things were getting out of hand and decided to weed them out. Unfortunately they weeded out the only flower as well as all the weeds and the Blue Pencils were no more.

All the members of the disbanded concert parties were at first posted off to a variety of regiments before being later amalgamated into The Central Pool of Artists which itself was then renamed Stars in Battle-Dress.

I was posted back to a Birmingham unit of the RASC at Drayton Manor at Fazeley near Tamworth, which meant going back into the Army for real, although I was put in charge of entertainments. I had to do my share of soldiering, and spent many an hour driving on

**There was a little man and he had a little gun and his bullets were made of liqourice**
**he shot a little duck in the parson's nose and it went straight through to the vicarage**

convoys, even if I was mainly trying to think up gags as I motored.

Sadly for a time all the concert parties stopped. But I put on a weekly show called Canteen Night. The lads couldn't go out every night. They were only allowed out one night a week. We put on some entertainment for them to keep them together so they wouldn't clear off and go absent without leave.

I used to involve fellers that were new, who were a little bit skittish and would be off given half a chance. I used to try to involve them in the show and grab their interest, and after a time that kept them together so we didn't have half the people running off. It gave them an interest and it kept them on the camp.

They weren't great actors by any means they were just lads having a bit of fun. I wrote sketches and organised competitions but I was also kept busy going down to London to do radio broadcasts. I was Gunner Smith

Entertains, Private Smith Entertains, I was always being called in on the radio. I think my advantage over so many of the other comics was that they could trust me to be clean.

I did a lot of gags and I've always said that, in life, you can get things done better by having a laugh about it in a humorous way than by complaining grumpily and being a pain in the neck.

We were always very short of ammunition. When we went out on manoeuvres, the Colonel said we had no ammunition to waste and we would have to improvise. Half of us hadn't got any guns anyway, so we went off as red team and blue team and, when we approached one of the enemy, we were supposed to put our fingers together just as you did as a little boy and go: "Bang, bang. You're dead!"

We were under the strictest orders to be serious about this play-acting but some of us found that rather difficult. This young officer jumped out on me and went: "Bang, bang. You're dead!" I kept walking. Again he went: "Bang, bang. You're dead!" I kept walking.

He ran up to me and said: "Bang, bang. You're dead! I have killed you twice, you should be dead now."

I said: "Oh no I shouldn't. Can't you hear me going tick tick, I'm a tank." War was a situation you made fun of. You had to. It was the only way to survive.

Then there was the gag where a sentry recounts a night-time encounter. He says: "Someone was approaching so I said, 'Halt who goes there.' He said 'Friend' so I shot him. "You shot him," says his mate. "Yes. He's not one of ours if he says 'Friend'. Ours say, 'Mind your own bloody business and come straight in.'

They were silly gags but they were right for the times.

Humour is a wonderful way to get your point across. Soon after I arrived at Drayton Manor I found it could be particularly effective. The camp was surrounded by woods and many of the soldiers under me were very inexperienced young conscripts who had never seen a rifle let alone held one.

It so happened that I was guard commander on a night when one of these young lads was on duty at the main gates. I clearly heard a voice call out: "Halt! Who goes there?" which seriously was the accepted challenge. There was no answer but the next thing I heard was a gunshot ring out.

**Hitler would have sent gas bombs over if we hadn't all had gas masks. This Civil Defence official went to deliver masks to a small cottage occupied by three spinsters - Mary, Annie and Fanny. Mary and Annie took their masks but the other one wasn't in. The official was just walking away when one of them shouted out: "What about our Fanny's?" The official snorted: "Just think yourselves lucky you've got one for your faces."**

In a Britain filled with rumours of a possible German invasion, the sound of a gunshot at night-time was quite frightening. I roused the rest of the guard and we dashed down to the main gate to investigate.

The young solder was standing, white-faced with his rifle still pointing towards the woods. "It's over there, Corporal," he told me, trembling with fear. "Over there in the woods, there is somebody there!"

We searched immediately and the guard made such a good job of scouring the woods that I wouldn't be surprised if it didn't result in a generation being missed in the local rabbit population! But there was nobody there.

The young sentry had been alarmed by the moon shining in the trees, which were swaying in the night's breeze. And suffering from the nerves of his first night on guard he had shot at shadows.

Our commanding officer, the camp major, was away at the time and the Adjutant of the Day was a rather finicky fellow who came down demanding to know what was going on.

When I explained what had happened he took immediate action. He decided to take all the ammunition away from the guards so this mistake could not happen again.

I thought this was a singularly daft move, even for an officer. The atmosphere at the time was one of high tension as an invasion was widely anticipated. But I said nothing at the time.

I just planned a little guard sketch for the next in our series of camp concerts, when in our audience were had all our officers, including the lieutenant who had so effectively disarmed the camp guards.

In this sketch I introduced a gag or two, and I played a guard carrying a toasting fork instead of a bayonet. And then one of the others, dressed as an officer, stalked on stage and demanded of the guard: "What are you doing? What is the fork for?"

"Well, sir. It's what the Sergeant Major said."

"What did he say?"

"He said, 'Make toast' sir!"

"Well he didn't. He said: 'Take post!'"

There followed a few more gags in that line until I shouted:"Halt! Who goes there? Now come on! Don't mess about! Halt! Who goes there? If you don't stop I'll go down to the guardroom for a bullet."

Naturally this brought the house down but our Major was mystified and astounded because he hadn't a clue what everyone was laughing at. It certainly didn't sound very funny to him and he was a man with a keen sense of humour. He immediately instituted inquires and two days later that Adjutant was posted and the guards had ammo in their rifles again. That's the power of a good laugh.

We used to have competitions. One favourite was a quiz, with teams made up from drivers, NCOs, and officers. I used to put the questions together. Some were straightforward questions and others were trick questions.

We were unlucky enough to get a Sergeant Major who had been working on the railways at New Street Station in Birmingham. A big, big man, he was basically a bully. He caused so much trouble among the lads. For some reason the lads looked to me to put things right.

I had a personal reason for taking him down a peg or two after he had me on a charge just because I hadn't had anybody on a charge. I wouldn't let anyone go out of the camp at night unless they looked clean and tidy with their boots shining and smart. I was the Corporal in charge of the camp police.

This Sergeant Major had me up in front of the Major just because I had not punished anyone. I said: "Can I just ask, sir, if anyone has been brought in from the town because they are improperly dressed? Because they don't get past me, sir, unless they look smart and their boots are clean. Could you walk out of this room and have a good look all around the camp and see if there is any litter, because I think you'll find there isn't. If I see anybody drop anything I make them go round the camp and pick up all the other rubbish, so they don't drop litter.

**We've got a new officer. He's so stupid even the other officers have noticed.**

The major pooh-poohed my charge and said 'forget it'. But this fellow had his knife into me after that because I had shown him up for what he was, a bloody idiot. A few nights later I was organising one of my quizzes and this Sergeant Major came up to me and said: "I want to be in the officers' team tonight Waddington."

I said: "You're not an officer sir, you're an NCO." "They're one short," he barked gruffly, "I'll go in with them." There was no stopping him so I decided to set a special question up just for him. Bearing in mind we were a motor transport unit and our job was to work out journeys and travel, it shouldn't have been too difficult.

I said: "We will now assume that Tamworth from Fazeley is two miles. A man drove off in a wagon from Fazeley to go to Tamworth. He travels three times faster in the first part of the journey than in the third part of the journey and it takes him one hour. What is his average speed?"

He said: "Can you say that again?" I repeated it. He puzzled for a moment and then he snarled angrily: "That's not a fair question." I said: "All right, I'll pass it over to the drivers." They burst out laughing and said: "Two miles in an hour, that's two miles an hour." And the audience were all laughing at this big fool. The Major was there and he looked at this berk and thought 'what a dimwit'. And he was posted three days later. They got rid of him.

Taking the mickey always works better than complaining. Any time ENSA shows came I had to look after them. Some of them were very good. We had that wonderful Welsh actor Emlyn Williams and Night Must Fall and some other marvellous acts, but we also had a lot of very second-rate people who were doing their best for the War Effort - the German War Effort it seemed at the time. I felt sorry for them.

At one concert we had a rather large visiting lady singer to entertain us. She must have been about 15 stone but she had quite a nice contralto voice. But when she started singing: "I'm a little bird," a fellow from the back shouted: "I wouldn't like to clean your cage out". It brought the house down. I felt so sorry for the poor woman but it was the best laugh of the night by a mile.

I was still doing quite a lot of broadcasts from Fazeley. They used to let me go down and do Ack-Ack Beer-Beer, the anti-aircraft barrage balloon show. I think I did more appearances on those than anybody else. I used to go once a fortnight or three weeks and this got the Sergeant Major's back up as well. But the rest of the lads used to like me going as well because I

> I know a sub-Lieutenant
> with eyes of shiny blue
> he used to knit me jumpers
> and make such lovely stew
> his hair is nice and wavy
> he wears such gorgeous clothes
> I don't know what they call him
> but we think he's one of those.

used to get paid about seven guineas, and we could all have a night out on that.

When I was drafted into Stars in Battle-Dress it was a very very exciting part of my life, a part of my life that really made me think. We had a common enemy, things weren't all roses by any means, you had to make fun of adversity - and that is both my way and the British way.

I was working in other concert parties, and we did a tour of the north-east of England, entertaining troops in places like Catterick and Newcastle. It was a rehearsal really for the work we would be doing after the invasion of Europe took place. We were very closely watched by the powers that be to make sure our shows were up to scratch. We were doing two or three shows a day and then going back to sleep on the floor of the Newcastle barracks at night. We were just learning to do our job.

The changing facilities at our shows were rarely anything to go to your head. Certainly, members of the concert party never wasted much time arguing over who had the largest dressing room. Usually that was because we were all in the same boat, or cowshed, or corner of the village hall.

More than once we had to change behind a swiftly-draped blanket. We parked our lorry for one concert at the bottom of a field that sloped down to our 'stage' like a natural theatre. This Colosseum was somewhere in deepest Hertfordshire. It was a lovely summer's evening and the troops all sat down on the grass. They let all the ATS girls come right to the front so they could get a decent view.

To make a changing room we strung out ropes from the side of this three-ton lorry and hung Army blankets. We had rigged up curtain on the back of the lorry which was to be our stage.

I stripped off behind one blanket and I was totally nude getting ready for the show. Suddenly I heard gales of laughter from behind me. At first I thought this lot are a good audience, we haven't even started yet.

But when I looked round I could see that the blanket had fallen down. My naked rear end was the source of all the unscripted amusement. As quickly as I could I rushed round behind the back of the lorry out of sight. I was embarrassed but I knew they wouldn't recognise me when I went on the stage because I was wearing so much make-up I looked older than I do now.

When I did get on I couldn't resist making a reference. "What did you think of Mr Bottomley earlier on?" I said. "What a cheek!"

I wasn't a pro. I was an amateur. But I was happy to let people believe I was a professional because I had decided that was what I wanted to be after the War.

Later there was an influx of ENSA people who wanted to help the War effort but they did not find it very easy to go among tough lads who were involved in the fighting.

While I was stationed at Fazeley one of our big trips out was to the Perry Bar greyhound track in Birmingham. For a while things were not going well for us and we couldn't afford to come away losing - not on Army pay. So we developed this system. Sevens, I called it. We would back number six and number one to come in first and second and then we would reverse the bet, and then move on to number five and number two. Usually it seemed to pay off and we began to come away with a bit of money. But at one day everything we backed came nowhere. I've never had such a disastrous day we had no luck at all.

We were doing so badly I said, 'I wouldn't back the hare in the next race' and do you know in the very next race there was a technical

> **If you wanted any equipment you went to the Quartermaster. I went in once and asked: "Have you got a pair of pincers?" "Take my two assistants," came the quick reply.**

fault and the hare went flying up in the air halfway round the circuit. They had to re-run that race and it went wrong again. We looked on in amazement, I could have got fantastic odds on that happening.

A little later, our unit was transferred from Drayton Manor to another camp about 10 miles away where the headquarters was another requisitioned manor house. And at our new home I was introduced to the dubious delights of an intensive course of Commando training.

Among the exhaustive list of tests I was expected to pass as a junior NCO was leading my small section to capture the camp HQ after

> Two sailors were marooned on a desert island after their ship was torpedoed.They had been there about two months and they were really bored with their situation when one day one of them suggested a game of "Who Am I?" The other agreed and the first man went on: "I'm 5ft 6in, I'm blonde, I've got blue eyes, and a 38inch bust. Who Am I? " The second sailor said: "I don't give a damn. Come here and give us a kiss."

being taken miles away in a sealed three-tonner truck. We were dropped off with a map reference from the unsmiling referee who then left us to make our way back as best we could.

On this particular night several sections were dropped at different points and varying distances from the camp. Our hands and faces were all blacked up and the game as to get back without being detected by any of the referees taking part.

Luckily I had learned in advance that the refs were from a Welsh unit and, using my very best imitation of a squaddie from the land of our fathers, I managed to trick our little team's way past and our section managed to capture our base.

But we were desperate men and no mistake. At one point during our night's travels we hid behind a row of terraced houses to escape detection and then quietly let ourselves, all 13 of us fully blacked up, in at the back door of a tiny home and trooped out the front with just a 'Good evening' for the astonished occupants before disappearing into the night.

## Chapter Five

# D-Day

When I was eventually transferred from
general duties with the RASC to 'The
Central Pool of Artists', which later
became Stars in Battle-Dress, I found myself in
extremely good company. There were some
marvellous people in that talented unit,
including dear old Arthur Haynes, Charlie
Chester and Janet Brown.

In fact, Stars in Battle-Dress was a hot-bed of
talent, including Sid Milward and his Nitwits,
who included a very funny coloured boy called
Cyril Laguey. He was built like a shoelace and
will always be one of the funniest men I have
ever met. He was marvellous and once you got
him laughing, his own shrill laughter was so
infectious that everyone laughed with him.
Terry-Thomas and Harry Secombe were also
there. I was delighted to be thought worthy of a
place with such illustrious company.

I went with Stars in Battle-Dress to tour the
camps in the North East, all round Newcastle-
upon-Tyne, Sunderland and on the other side of
the country - even up as far as Carlisle -
entertaining the troops in what turned out to be
a very good concert party indeed.

We were based in Newcastle, where we
were found digs in private homes. It would

> The cost of living's far too high
> said little Mrs Brown.
> The tailors charge too much for clothes.
> Their trousers should come down.

have been difficult for us to have been billeted in a camp because frequently, we were not able to turn in before some unearthly hour like two or three in the morning, and were consequently allowed to sleep late. With the troops normally having to be back in camp by 23.59 hours and having to be up at reveille at 0600, mixing us together would not have worked. Because we were living or lodging with families, the troops thought the Stars in Battle-Dress were getting real 'star' treatment, but we weren't.

Very probably we got far less rest and relaxation than they did. We certainly got fewer leave passes! For instance, when Christmas came along, we entertainers were not allowed home because our services were required at the various camp concerts.

I managed to get home only once in six years at Christmas time and then I had only just got off the train when I received a telegram. It read: "Come back. We need you for Christmas." You'd have thought I was a turkey!

By the winter of 1944 we were living with almost daily rumours of our imminent invasion. There was a national feeling that, after five years of being on the receiving end of the worst the German war machine could deliver, we were at last about to hit back in a big way. But the big question was 'When?'

The authorities insisted on total security but with thousands upon thousands of troops stationed all the way round the south coast, that was difficult. As hundreds of all kinds of boats were busily prepared for the crossing so four little Stars in Battle-Dress concert parties were despatched to a Folkestone camp ready for embarkation.

No-one knew why we were at that particular camp at that particular time. But we all had a very good idea.

No-one was allowed to leave camp because of the desperate attempts to keep the imminent invasion of France secret. We were each issued with a special food kit in a box about 10 inches square, by three or four inches deep. That was your rations for a day or two! Everything in the box was cleverly condensed.

There was even a tiny cooker made up of a piece of material which burned on its own little metal holder. And while condensed concentrated porridge, tea and sugar tasted terrible, at least it was something to eat - and something to hang onto when you reached the other side of the English Channel.

But as the waiting went on, we did have a lot of spare time on our hands in the Folkestone camp. We had parades to attend, with the Scots Guards, the regiment we were to cross with. But in our leisure time we gave shows to the troops in our tented coastal city. As spring wore on and the weather improved, the feeling of anticipation grew. Yet it was hard to comprehend we were soon to be plunged from the idyllic English countryside into the horrors of war.

Cyril Laguey was in my little group and his ability to get humour out of anything was quite remarkable. But I thought he had pushed it a little too far the day he started clowning on parade. The Scots Guards Major was not a tall man, but he was built like a tank. I don't think you could have found a rounded part of him anywhere. He was totally square and pure soldier from the top of his Glengarry right down to the very tips of his glistening, toe-capped Army boots.

Slim Cyril was supposed to be standing with us ready for inspection. But unlike conventional soldiers he was not wearing a single piece of equipment! Back-pack, side-pack, weapon pouches, straps, belt, the lot was all draped round his feet!

The Major strode smartly over to him and sharply told Cyril: "Pick that lot up!" Cyril began to mimic the common conception of the subservient coloured man's whine and replied: "Ah just cain't boss. Ah just cain't boss." It was hilarious but I'm afraid the Major did not even begin to see the joke.

**Mae West walked into our hut last night. All the privates stood up.**

He demanded: "Pull yourself together man. What are you going to do when you get over the other side?"

And Cyril, eyes rolling, wailed on: "Dat's what's a-worryin' me boss. Dat's what's a-worryin' me!" When he acted this way you couldn't get cross with him because he was so funny. The entire parade was in fits of suppressed laughter. The Major looked as though steam would come out of his head and walked away in amazement.

We spent many a peaceful afternoon after lunch playing poker in one of the massive marquees that had been erected as canteens. None of us were great gamblers, but we enjoyed the sport of the game. It provided a much-needed release from the tension of waiting.

Arthur Haynes, yours truly and several of the other lads would gather round and lay a blanket on the ground as a makeshift card table. We certainly did not have much money and were betting only in halfpennies and pennies - the old variety at that - at most.

Occasionally the stakes built up and a lucky winner could find himself picking up as much as five shillings, some 25 pence in the new-fangled money. Which seemed like an enormous windfall. If you could find them, you could buy yourself a couple of packets of cigarettes and still have enough left for a night out on the beer.

I was never surprised that Arthur went on to have such a successful career as a comedian after the War. He was a wonderful character and a great joker. One afternoon he dealt out the cards and when I picked up my hand I got an enormous shock.

I looked down to see that I had four kings and a nine. Anyone who has played poker will appreciate what a magnificent hand it was. I tried my hardest to keep the elation out of my face. I stayed poker-faced, as they say, and did my best to pretend I was reluctantly pushing the boat out on a pure whim.

> The air raid siren goes and an elderly couple rush out of their house to the shelter. Suddenly the wife rushes back. "Where are you going Annie?" says the husband. "I'm going for my teeth," says the wife. "For Goodness sake, they're dropping bombs not fish and chips."

Strangely, so did everyone else! The stakes in the middle rose along with my blood pressure as I anticipated that tidy pile of pennies and halfpennies transferring itself to my pocket. I thought to myself: "This is fantastic. Surely no-one can possibly beat me now."

Just as I felt I would burst with joy, the bugle sounded for us all to go on parade and we had no option but to finish the game there and then. Supremely confident of total success I told the others: "Come on. We had better put our hands down and whoever has the best hand takes the money." So with everyone in complete agreement, we laid down our hands face upwards.

I looked proudly down at my four kings and was then astonished to see the fellow next to me had four queens, a chap on the far side of the blanket had four jacks, somebody else had four tens, but Arthur Haynes, who had dealt the cards, was beaming down at a hand of four aces!

Arthur was always a great joker and he had set up the cards during our lunchtime break. As realisation dawned we all scrabbled to grab our money back as we laughed at the trick. It was great fun, and so typical of Arthur. He even took it in good part when we gave him a bit of a toss in the blanket to get our own back.

Eventually the time for D-Day came. After all the secrecy and false starts we certainly raised a cheer or two when the first wave of Allied forces landed successfully on June 6th.

We went over a few days later. In fact we made our crossing soon after June 10, my 28th birthday. The flight from Dunkirk had been a disaster and yet it was wonderful the way we got people out. It was unbelievable the way soldiers made it home in anything from Navy boats to beer barrels, virtually.

I think I knew then that the Germans could never defeat that sort of spirit. The British people have great strength of character. We never know when we're beaten. However tough it gets, we always carry on.

As we were in the final moments before embarkation I realised we were with some lads who had been through Dunkirk. And they were leading us into all saying: "Right. It's our turn now."

And we went all the way across the Channel on these motor torpedo boats, bouncing up and down like beach balls. They were diesel-driven and the smell of the diesel and the movement in the water made a lot of the lads very very sick.

As we travelled down the Channel from Folkestone, going round the safe side of the Isle of Wight to avoid detection by the Germans, a lot of the lads on board, Arthur Haynes among them, were very ill.

They were mostly down in the bottom but I wouldn't go down. I stayed on deck. I had done a lot of horse riding and I think that helped. I just rode it like I would a horse.

On deck they had a great heap of tins of soup lashed down under a sheet of canvas. In

There was a young man of Devizes
who had ears of two different sizes.
One was so small it was no good at all
the other was a bloody great big 'un!

the middle of each of the tins there was a wick
with gun cotton in. You lit this and, as it burned
down, it heated your soup. I loved this soup
and I had four tins because so many of my
mates were too ill to face food of any kind. In
fact, some of them looked so bad it seemed as
though they would never face food again.

They were in quite a bad state. It was a
wonder some of them could walk let alone fight
when they got over. But I thought to myself: "If
I'm going to be sick, then at least I'll make sure I
have something to be sick on."

We came ashore and immediately began to
foot-slog it towards our destination, Bayeux. In
spite of our endless briefings, none of us
seemed quite able to remember exactly how far
we had to walk and, loaded like packhorses
with all our equipment and weapons, we
seemed to be on a never-ending march.

I clutched my most precious possession
closely to me. That was my beloved banjo-

ukulele in a specially constructed and strengthened case. I had refused point-blank to part with that. I hung on to my uke like grim death.

After trudging our first kilometre or so we hitched a lift on a passing DUKW, one of the large amphibious vehicles which proved to be one of the keys to the successful invasion.

I was pleased to get away from the beach. My first footsteps on French soil were anything but relaxing. The whole wide expanse of sand was a melee of men and machinery struggling to sort themselves out under intermittent shellfire from the Germans. Our Navy was offshore in the Channel shelling over our heads and the noise and horror of war hit me for the very first time.

After four years of clowning my way up the Army entertainment ladder, I suddenly realised that I was well within range of my most hostile audience to date. Years later when an officious Inland Revenue official rudely asked me if I owned any property abroad, I tartly told him there was a certain section of French beach I had claimed in the name of freedom a generation or so before, but I don't think he quite took my point.

There were troops, tanks, armoured vehicles, guns and frenzied activity all around us. We had a bird's eye view of things as we rode along the little lanes away from the Channel on top of this DUKW. There was an enormous feeling of elation and achievement. We were there. We had made it across the Channel and we were in the thick of the Normandy invasion that would start the important process of liberating Europe from the occupying German forces.

The ride was much appreciated, a very attractive alternative to walking. We stopped that first night in a village called Sommerview where we found an old bombed out monastery. We went down into the basement in search of a billet.

At that time the Allies had only just secured their Second Front foothold. They still occupied only a tiny perimeter strip of northern France and the Germans were battling hard to push us back into the sea. They were giving us Hell and in return our guns were giving them a good pasting.

That explained the devastated state of the monastery. Even so, we still found odd rooms and corners where we could bed down for the night and cover ourselves with a few blankets. The German troops had only recently been using the place as a billet themselves and there were still some serviceable beds we could use.

The six of us were a very tight little team. We were all mates. There was Biff Byfield and his orchestra, as they called him, who played the clarinet; an Italian singer called Phil Sicco; a comedy cartoonist who was good, even if I can't remember his name; and a very good pianist who had worked in Denmark Street. I used him for a few comedy routines. The feeling of all having a common enemy was the feeling that bound us together.

I think I was a better comedian than I would have been a soldier. I felt, and I still feel, that I had been given a very very responsible job. There were only 30 men who came over in the invasion to entertain all those hundreds of thousands of troops. And we had to do it at the first possible chance. We were split into our five units of six men to try to make the men forget the horrors just for an hour or so. Otherwise I think they would have just gone mad.

By and large we all pulled for each other, there was no bad feeling. The only time we didn't, in my experience, was when I had a dust-up with the Italian singer in our party, Signor Sicco.

That could have been very nasty because he came at me with a knife after I made a joke about the Italian Army not being exactly the world's fiercest fighting force. As he came at me I just managed to get hold of his arm and turn the knife away from me.

I couldn't hit him because I was an NCO so I just grabbed him as tight as I could until he calmed down. I had to stop him stabbing me. Mind you, I think I did fracture two of his ribs. For some reason he didn't bother me any more after that!

We saw some amazing sights that summer in France. I'll never forget, one day in Normandy, we came across the strangely comical sight of two bow-legged little Lancashire Fusiliers marching along with about 20 strapping German prisoners-of-war. The contrast in size was so funny but the two squaddies were determined. For those Germans, the War was definitely over.

Cyril Laguey was no less offbeat and amusing as we went into action than he had been back on the Folkestone parade ground. He steadfastly refused to enter our new home. For

**There was a fellow from the Royal Artillery who went home on leave. He was sitting by the fire reading his newspaper and he had had a long journey so he was just dozing off. They had one of those big kitchen ranges and as he fell asleep his paper caught alight. Just then his wife came in and when she saw what was happening she yelled 'Fire!' He leaps out of the chair, throws the cat into the oven, and shouts: "Number One gun ready, Sir!"**

some strange reason, he was scared stiff of the spirits that inhabited the place and he found a highly individual shelter of his own.

Part of our equipment for our concert parties were four mini-pianos, packed in sturdy wooden boxes for the trip. Soon after our arrival at Sommerview we unpacked the pianos and left their travelling boxes outside the monastery. They were about four feet square and three feet deep. It was into one of these boxes that Cyril insisted on crawling. To him these cramped sleeping quarters were infinitely preferable to a night in an old monastery.

After night fell, we were all dog-tired so we decided to turn in for the night. We went into the ruined monastery and the nooks and crannies where we had found room enough to make a bed.

Cyril stayed outside and curled up for the night in his chosen box. It must have been like trying to get to sleep in a coffin and Cyril thought that was exactly what it might become as German shelling started to pepper our new home.

The clatter of shrapnel on his box was enough to have Cyril rushing in to join us. Somehow he forget his fears of the ghosts of the place in an instant. Cyril was a real card, a natural funny man. I thought about getting him working for me after the War but it never came to anything. He's the only bloke I've ever met who has never failed to make me laugh. He could make anything seem funny.

From that old monastery I witnessed the biggest bombing raid of the war, the massive bomber raid on the town of Caen. We watched, transfixed, at the sight of wave after wave of our bombers, with fighter backing, filing the night sky. They seemed to be overhead for ever, pouring down their deadly cargo of bombs on the stumbling block of Caen. Even 15 miles away the monastery shook as the hundreds of tons of explosives rained down.

The Germans were very well entrenched in Caen and were fortified in every direction. So we flattened the town. The Germans had gone by the time the bombs started dropping but the destruction was still necessary to allow the Allied advance to proceed.

Within two or three days of that I was in the wreckage of the town up on a makeshift stage trying to do a show for the Allied troops who had just moved in. The only building I could see that hadn't been hit was the hospital. It had a few pock marks on the walls but it was substantially intact, which was astonishing if you had seen what a pasting the place had taken.

I've never seen anything like it. The place was flattened. We were looking for somewhere to put on a show. A military policeman came to our aid. He showed us down some steps to a huge cellar which was ideal and we put on quite a few shows down there. I gave him one of the cards I'd had printed. It was designed to look like a playing cards - the Ace of Hearts.

After the War he married a New Zealand girl and went to live over there. He is the one chap I would love to have seen for my *This is Your Life* years later, but that's another story.

But there was always humour along with danger. I recall when we were doing hand

> I said to our Sergeant Major, 'I pray for you
> every night.' He said, 'Do you? Why, thank
> you very much.' I said, 'No, don't thank me.
> You're still here.'

grenade training, learning how to throw the deadly things. It's a good idea to be some distance away when they explode, but the chap next to me hurled his straight up in the air and we really scattered before it landed.

I realise how lucky I am to be here. There are thousands of lads with every bit as much right to be here as me who are buried on foreign soil.

When we first arrived in France our little cardboard boxes of grub were invaluable. You could put your dixie on your tripod and cook up your Quaker Oats. It wasn't exactly home cooking but it kept us going. There were enough packets of stuff in that for the first couple of days.

Then as we secured a foothold in France we started fending for ourselves. We used to go up to French farmhouses and trade a few pieces of chocolate for some potatoes. Once we bought seed potatoes and they tasted awful.

When I was really hungry I swopped an old pair of boots for a duck. Being a former butcher's boy I knew how to cook it all right but I think I made the mistake of sharing it with too many people because there only seemed to be a mouthful of meat each.

In my humble experience, the correct number of people for a duck supper has always been just two. That is you and the duck!

We never seemed to have much money so some of us developed the occasional wheeze to supplement the miserable Army pay. Stealing and selling Government property is, of course, a very serious offence, especially if you're serving in the armed forces when you do it.

My own little trick was to go on stage wearing an old pair of size eight Army boots, even though my proper size was a seven. The boots I wore on stage always had great holes in the bottoms and I used to crack a few jokes about Quarter-masters.

I would show the audience the soles of both my boots and say. "Do you know something? The soles on these boots are so thin that if I stood on a sixpence I could tell you whether it was heads or tails."

Once, after the show, the Quarter-master came up to me and asked: "Is that really the best pair of boots you've got?"

I replied: "It's the ONLY pair of boots I've got!" The Quarter-master then reluctantly issued me with a new pair of size eights, which were always the best size to sell. That's how I got that duck.

Shafts of humour let in a little light to the gloom of wartime. And even the oldest jokes can be brought up to date. The old Army method of passing on messages was one good example. In The First World War there was the famous story of a message that started out as: "Send us reinforcements, we are going to advance." That was mangled into: "Send us three and fourpence, we are going to a dance."

Our version involved the widespread rumour that the German General Rommel had been captured in the Middle East. The message started life as: "Rommel captured. Send a bus," but was strangely converted into: "Camel ruptured. Send a truss."

While these were dark and dangerous days for all of us, we were lifted and kept going by the camaraderie between us all. There was such a mixture of folk. Ordinary working blokes rubbed shoulders with fellows from very well-to-do families who did not want to be officers. We were drawn together by this common enemy and we were going to do him in. I don't think I ever had any real doubt about the eventual outcome.

One night we were struggling to find our way back to our camp-site just outside Caen when we stumbled across one of the more chilling stories of the war. We witnessed the opening of a mass grave in some woods nearby. Some 130 Canadian soldiers had come out of the woods to surrender to the Germans. They were outnumbered and surrounded and had no chance of fighting their way out. But the Germans made them dig their own graves and then killed them all. It was a dreadful thing.

The bodies were exhumed and the murdered Canadians each received a proper Christian burial.

Some of the French people took us into their homes to tell us what the Germans had been like. I will never forget being taken into one cellar to be shown walls pock-marked with bullets.

People had been taken down there and butchered as a reprisal after a German was killed. They would kill 10 or 20 people quite ruthlessly in cold blood. They were punishing people who had no reason to be punished. I simply cannot understand the mentality, I don't believe British soldiers would ever behave like that.

In spite of our role as entertainers we still felt very much part of the Army. I wasn't doing a job I had asked for. The Army had picked me out to entertain and I was determined to do it as effectively as I could. I knew I wasn't a coward so I didn't mind not being thrust into the frontline but I would always rather tell jokes to people than kill them! So I suppose I was happy with my lot. We were under orders to put on shows wherever you got the chance and that is what we did. And if you could make the lads laugh under those circumstances, it felt like a real achievement.

We had a three-ton Army lorry, and, often with yours truly at the wheel, we would trundle round behind our frontline trying to bring a bit of entertainment wherever we went. The little lanes of coastal Normandy were always brimming with troops and people moving along in anything from tiny carts to tanks.

We used to do shows on the back of lorries, in cowsheds, anywhere we could find. And it certainly taught you about timing. I was always thinking, I must get the end of this gag in before

**When I was just a little boy
I asked my father:"What will I be?
Will I be handsome?
Will I be tall?
He said: "No you'll be bald, like me."**

that truck hurtles past and drowns me out.

We were spared a lot of the day-to-day discipline because of our special job. We didn't often have to worry about going on parade or concern ourselves with having too many kit inspections. We knew we had to keep ourselves smart and be a credit to the Army.

On our few nights off we went to the casino or the local dog track or even sometimes to visit French people. Most of the locals seemed very pleased to see us, although there were some isolated cases of women sniping out of their windows at us.

But the French took their own bitter revenge on the women they thought had been collaborating the Germans. I had been in France about a fortnight when, in Lion-sur-Mer, I witnessed the shocking spectacle of French women, with their heads crudely shaved by their liberated countryfolk, being herded down streets like cattle and being completely ridiculed by an angry crowd howling abuse. Sticks and stones were hurled at them by many of the youngsters. I didn't enjoy watching at all. Those women might have got what some people regarded as their just desserts, but it was not a very edifying experience. The locals were really vicious. They just degraded these women completely.

We had many a happier night out, visiting the local bars and drinking Calvados. That particular local delicacy is an apple brandy that is some sort of a relative to the scrumpy with which I originally kick-started my career in showbusiness. The stuff they sold us in those little bistros certainly packed a punch. It could just about blow off your head and, in fact, it did make many of our troops very ill indeed.

I might have been married but I didn't feel it. My mind was made up by this time. At the end of the War I would look round for a bride I could really love. Evelyn had already been consigned to the past in my thoughts. I simply wanted to get out of the marriage as cleanly as possible.

I didn't feel at all guilty about making the occasional visit to the brothel in Bayeux. This was wartime, remember. People were separated for years on end. Don't tell me all those young women left alone while their husbands were in, say, Burma for maybe three years, went without for all that time.

I'm sure lots of them cared really deeply for their missing partners but the thought would occur in their minds, 'I wonder if he is being faithful all this time'. People are only human after all. The War was an extraordinary experience for everyone involved. They all coped with it as best they could but many people did things that would otherwise never have happened.

There was enormous pressure to go astray on men and women, and that is why I think the brothels were just one way of helping people to cope. I don't believe there is anything wrong with it. It helped to make sure our soldiers weren't going with tramps and picking up all sorts of dangerous diseases.

And on an emotional level it caused a minimum upset because they could go back home knowing they hadn't met anyone else that they wanted to marry and wreck their home life or anything like that. A lot of marriages did break down as a direct result of

A mother goes in to her soldier son's bedroom
and shouts: "You're late for work."
The son says: "I'm not going. I've got two
good reasons why I'm not going into work
today. The other blokes keep bashing me
and I hate the Army." His mum answers:
"I've got two good reasons why you are
going to work. You're 37 years of age.
And you are the commanding officer."

the War, they were just another sad casualty I'm afraid.

The girls in the brothel were in their early to mid twenties. There was an older woman in charge and it was all very relaxed. You could go in and have a drink, have a bit of a chat. And have a bird if you fancied it. But there again, it didn't matter if you didn't indulge. There was no pressure on the customers but the attraction was there. Being young and virile men, as we were, it was a natural course of events.

I believe, in the circumstances of war, it has a place. Of course, if this had all been the other way round and the wives had been at the front with a string of fellows, then I don't know what their husbands would have thought. This was long before the ideas of sexual equality that exist today and I know I'm probably guilty of double standards. This was one-sided but that's just the way I see things. These lads were under tremendous pressure in other ways. I think a few visits to the local brothel were totally acceptable.

I'm not saying it is the greatest thing that happened in the War, I just believe it was right and very necessary. When you think you might die the next day, it does tend to concentrate your mind a little.

The lads needed solace. They were away from their wives and loved ones facing up to death day and night. They were better going to these very well-run brothels than going off looking for women and all sorts of things happening. It happened in Normandy, not in Britain where men were expected to wait for sex until they went home on leave.

I think the brothels saved a lot of marriages. They provided a very necessary release for the men. These girls were examined every day to make absolutely sure they were clean and free from disease. The local doctor had to visit them every day. The British Army knew what was happening but they turned a blind eye to it. I think our medical officers got certain assurances from the French medical officers as to what the inspection routine entailed. They were determined to prevent any of our fellows getting diseases and taking them back home.

The one I visited was just on the outskirts of Bayeux. It was run like a club. You could just go in and have a drink if you wanted to. But it was spotlessly clean and very well run. There were these beautiful girls walking around and if you fancied one, you went up to her, gave her a nod and the two of you went upstairs. The bedrooms were just above the club. The girls all washed beforehand and the men all had to wear a condom.

It certainly wasn't very expensive, even on a soldier's pay. I never saw any officers there, it was just for the ranks, this place. There were about 100 francs to the £1 in those days and the girls charged about 25 francs a time. It was very reasonable.

I went three times in three months. With the lads, we all had a good laugh and then paid our money. I'm not ashamed of it. This was wartime. We all knew that you had to live for today because you might be dead tomorrow.

I had never experienced anything like it in my life. There were certainly no places like that back in my native Oldham. And my mother had been very strict with me where the opposite sex was concerned. Even well into my twenties I knew very very little about women. She kept me tightly wrapped up in that respect.

When I was a grown man and working for her in the butcher's business, if ever I had a day off - which wasn't very often - she never liked me to take a girl to the pictures. I did as I was told so I was a bit backward where the opposite sex was concerned. So when I went into this brothel with a bunch of mates I was completely flabbergasted.

**Have you heard about the Sergeant Major breaking his leg? Shut-up you idiot. It doesn't happen until tomorrow.**

I don't think there was anything wrong with brothels in wartime. It made men out of a lot of boys. Let's face it, without those women, a lot of those men would never have known what life was all about.

They were all professional ladies. There was nothing scruffy or rough about them and they weren't street walkers, because the Army wouldn't have stood for it if it hadn't been properly organised. I suppose many of these women would have had a flow of German clients before we arrived. I wouldn't question that at all, and I don't see that it matters.

From being a kid I wanted to make people laugh. I wasn't a dunce at school by any means but I was too interested in making people laugh. It was always the thing that gave me the biggest kick.

I was very upset for the kids in Normandy while the Germans had been in Occupation. They hadn't been properly fed. Kids would come up begging: 'Cigarette for Dadda, chocolate for mamma, you jig-a-jig Mamma for chocolate.' And they knew what they were saying as well.

Then we had a mess tent just outside Bayeux, and the kids would be delving into the swill bins. I couldn't bloody stand this and I went out and gave these kids nearly all the food I had off my plate. But that landed me in great trouble. The officer of the day spotted me and he went mad. He said: "Don't you realise what you're doing? There'll be crowds of them round here tomorrow. I know you feel sorry for them, we all feel sorry for them. But if you do that there'll be trouble."

He was right. The next day there were twice as many and they came looking for me. I said: "No. Big trouble for me." But it broke my heart. We ate well as soldiers but some of these kids hadn't seen a square meal in months.

When we got to Bayeux we did some shows in this old cinema which was designed just like Shakespeare's Globe Theatre. It was a simple circle and it was a very easy theatre to play. For the first Army show there, they brought some troops in. And there were some people in a box but I didn't know who the heck they were.

At the end of the show I said: "Well thank-you very much boys, it's been smashing working with you. I hope you have enjoyed the show. If you have, when you get back to the camp tell everybody you've seen the Stars in Battledress show directed by Captain George Black. If you didn't like it tell them it was ENSA.

I only found out later that the boss of ENSA was in the box!

The lifestyle was sometimes fairly basic. In one camp the only means of ablution we had was one tap in the middle of a field. Cyril the joker wandered over for a wash and did not notice the commanding figure of the Colonel waiting his turn for water.

He walked right past him without a salute or anything. This Colonel shouted at Cyril: "Do you know who I am?".

> Every Sunday we went on church parade. Protestants
> on the left, Catholics on the right, anyone else down the
> middle. There was just one chap in the middle.
> The Sergeant said:"What are you?"
> He said: "I'm a Sweden Borgian "
> "You what?" said the Sergeant to the soldier, who
> repeated it. "Well there's nowhere round here you can
> go," said the Sergeant."You had better go and clean the
> latrines."
> The following Sunday when we went on church parade
> this lad had joined the Catholics.The Sergeant shouted
> at him: "I thought you were a Sweden Borgian."
> The soldier looked up and said: "I don't like the place  of
> worship."

"No. Who are you?" said Cyril. "I am your Colonel," came the angry reply from the enraged officer. "Oh, I thought you was an ENSA man," squealed Cyril.

A month or so later they brought over one or two ENSA parties, and George Formby was in one of them. They did have good people. I knew Formby quite well. At one point he wanted to buy my uke and I wouldn't sell it to him. I had a better one than him. He was all right, George, but I couldn't say the same about his wife. George was a tremendous draw before the War.

Formby was a one-off, a unique performer. The big stars of those days and any days for that matter were all just one-offs. They didn't copy anybody. And that was what I determined to do. I didn't want to be like anybody else, I didn't want that at all. I worked on all sorts of ideas to be different.

I didn't sleep properly for about the first five weeks of the Occupation. What with all the noise - of people shouting, tanks and other heavy vehicles moving, land mines going off and the constant bombing and shelling - I suppose I just got out of the habit of having a good night's sleep.

I must have dozed off a few times but I could never sleep properly. I was still not a big drinker, and the only drink I would have appreciated was a drop of whisky. But there just wasn't any to be had. The Calvados was all right for those who developed a taste for it and could swig it back without too many ill effects, but it was a shade too heavy for my palate.

Then one evening I was doing a show with Biff Byfield, Frances Tanner and Phil Sicco. Suddenly, looking along the front row of the audience, I spotted a familiar face. The mystery soldier and I exchanged a look of mutual recognition but I still could not place him when afterwards he came back stage to meet me.

As soon as I saw him close to, I instantly recognised him - it was my cousin Walter. I had last seen him as a boy in Oldham. And my abiding memory was of going to his home for lunch when I was at Waterloo Street High School when he would always cadge my rice pudding from me!

He was younger than me and had only been a very small boy when I had last seen him, but he had heard of my entertaining career in the Army and had no difficulty identifying me up on stage.

Now he was in the same boat as me and it was wonderful to take a bit of time to reminisce about the old days. He invited me back to his mess which turned out to be a parked up three-ton lorry.

I do remember him saying: "We've got a drop of whisky if you would care to have a drink." I told him: "Would I like a drink? I would like a good night's sleep too. That whisky might help."

Some serious drinking went on that night and I found myself entertaining this strictly all-male assembly with a few "men's" stories. My last memory of this impromptu performance is of me standing with a pint pot held in one hand

and, while I was going through my repertoire, Cousin Walter pouring in more and more whisky.

As long as I talked, he kept pouring. As long as he poured, I kept talking.

Not surprisingly this evening was one of the very few occasions in my life when I became really drunk. However, with the singular exception of my stage debut at Gillingham, Dorset, whenever I've had a few too many I can always remember pretty well what has gone on. This gift of total alcoholic recall did not fail me, even on this monumental family-reunion drinking spree.

**"Halt! Who goes there?"**
**"Army chaplain."**
**"Advance Charlie and be recognised."**

For instance, I remember Cousin Walter and a fellow soldier insisting they escort me safely back to the farmhouse where I was billeted at the time. I remember we came to a ditch. I remember being told that on being given the command "Jump" we would all three jump the ditch together.

And I remember mistiming my jump and falling back into the water-filled ditch, dragging my two companions with me. I also remember with their help getting safely back to the farmhouse. But most of all I remember how ill I was once I got there!

When I woke up the next morning I discovered that I had been so sick during the night that one of the lads had put my head on the side of a biscuit tin that my mother had sent me over from home. My 'pillow' had left a terrible-looking, square indentation across one side of my face from the corner of the box. It took at least a month for that mark to gradually disappear.

But at least I had slept. And I was never kept awake worrying about the bombing again. The cycle of insomnia was broken by that bizarre drinking session and every night afterwards I slept like a log. At long last Cousin Walter had paid me back for his childhood rice pudding thefts.

**A pig is an animal born in Germany, fattened in France, slaughtered in Russian, salted in the Channel and canned in England.**

But as soon as we could, we started entertaining. We would use the corner of a field, an old farm building, anywhere. It was all very on the spur of the moment. One day we came across these troops and offered their Captain an hour's fun.

He was very keen for us to cheer up his men but he said: "Before you start we have been having a little bit of trouble with a German fighter pilot who keeps coming over and strafing our camp every evening at six o'clock."

We went off and had our food and pulled our lorry under some trees. Then I heard the noise of this 'plane coming and our boys had lined anti-aircraft guns at 500-yard spaces and they were waiting for him. Boom. That was the end of that German. "Right," said the Captain cheerily, "now let's have that concert."

Another time we set ourselves up in an apple orchard to entertain. In those days I always wore a very funny costume. I had a knitted bathing suit which hung right down on me - the crutch finished at my knees - a tin hat, these great big boots and my ukulele. And the ukulele had all coloured ribbons hanging off it. This outfit of many colours I was wearing, well, you could see it for miles.

This time we were just about to get on with the show on the back of a lorry when this young officer climbed up onto our makeshift stage and shouted to his men: "Now chaps, keep right under the trees, please. Keep well out of sight. You know the Germans will strafe anything they can see. So keep still and enjoy the show."

I listened to this speech from my position on the back of the lorry and I felt just like a dartboard. The show's drummer, who was a great big fellow, was perched with his equipment right at the back of the lorry. As the officer climbed down after making his happy announcement, I turned to look at the drummer and said: "Bloody Hell." He was shaking with equal mixtures of fear and laughter and promptly fell off, drums and all.

As usual I let the audience believe this latest disaster was all part of the programme. I looked round at my expectant public and said squeakily: "I won't be here long. I do a very quick act. Before you've had chance to hate me I've gone."

And that day I introduced what was literally a running gag. Every time I heard a plane I jumped smartly off the stage and rushed underneath the lorry. It got laughs every time.

So much humour came naturally out of the extraordinary circumstances. We were being fed and watered during a brief lull in hostilities in a reception area a few miles inland when I came across some more amusing material for my act.

CO had a beautiful wife who presented him with a
bouncing baby boy. On parade he said:
"Officers, NCOs and men of this regiment,
I would like to tell you my wife has this morning
presented me with a beautiful baby boy.
Officers NCOs and men, I thank you."
He never did find out who the father was.

There was a huge steaming bowl full of soup and another full of tea. You just had to go and help yourselves and then wash off your dishes in a bowl of hot washing-up water. We all enjoyed a laugh when we saw one of our lads was washing up his dixie in the tea urn. It was so weak you could hardly tell the difference.

There were only 30 of us to try to entertain all these millions of Allied soldiers, so we had our work cut out. We were all genuine serving soldiers. They dare not use civilian entertainers for fear they would be shot as spies if they were captured.

After Caen we pushed on across northern France. I did get to visit Paris for the first time but only on a weekend leave and the next place we paused for a while was Brussels, the Belgian capital. We did quite a few shows in a big ABC theatre. That is where I met up with Charlie Chester, who became a pal. He had got his hands on a Luger from a German and he wanted to get rid of it.

I said, 'I'll sell it for you' and I did. He had given 50 francs for it. I went to one of the fellows in the orchestra and offered it to him. His eyes widened when he saw this prized German gun. He paid 1,000 francs, which was what the weapon was really worth at that time, and he was well pleased. So was Charlie when I handed him the money. I said: "If you're going to get done for pinching it you'll have to have something to pay the fine."

Charlie was a great one for making up stories, and he invented a gag for me that still gets laughs today. I went bald before I was 23 and Charlie gave me the line: "I have tried everything to remedy my baldness. But I drew the line when this doctor told me to put a ferret up my nose to chase the hairs out."

I didn't find Bill Pertwee, who has since written his own book on Stars in Battle-Dress, to be nearly such a generous performer. He didn't mention me in his book, which miffed me a little as I was widely considered the Army's number one comedian. Soon after the War I was on the same bill as him at Bradford Alhambra and he was above me on that bill. I don't know why, I think he was in a regular radio programme or something.

A local businessman, who ran a big raincoat factory nearby, had booked the whole of the circle for his workers and he asked Bill Pertwee if he would just say a few words to them from out on stage. "Oh, I can't be doing with that," he said. "It will disrupt my act." They came to me and I happily agreed. I worked a line in teasing them for letting the rain in and afterwards the boss came backstage and invited my wife Lilian and I to lunch. He gave us both a beautiful raincoat, so exclusive it was only for sale in America.

That showed Bill Pertwee up. He could have had a nice raincoat if he'd only been a bit more cheerful. It doesn't do you any harm to do people a favour. I don't think Pertwee ever forgave me.

I found myself getting hardened to scenes of injury and death. Friends died but it was part of War. One of the things which saddened me the most was the way the animals suffered, particularly the horses. There were so many of the poor creatures killed by blasts, and with no-

"Now a little test about the Army," said the Sergeant
to a group of new recruits from all walks of life -
butchers, bakers, telegram boys, all sorts.
"Can anyone tell me what reveille is?"
"Yes Sergeant, that is when you blow the bugle and we
have to get up."
"Yes. Now, a 48-hour pass?"
"We can have two days away from the camp."
"Good. The last post?"
A lone voice piped up: "Five o'clock."

one available to shift the bodies, they were often
blown up by methane gas like big balloons and
occasionally they would explode and the stench
was dreadful.

Horses are remarkable creatures. Once they
have experienced a bombing raid and come
through unscathed, they are not frightened of
the next one. They ignore it and carry on
grazing. War is immensely sad for people, but
somehow the plight of dead and injured
animals always got to me as well.

There are so many sad scenes in my
memories. I remember on Carpiquet Airfield,
we were doing a show in an area between some
of the hangars. One of our lads was dancing
around and doing a soft shoe shuffle routine on
the ground and a German soldier's foot came
up. His movements lifted it out of the soil and

we found a whole lot of bodies there, just shallow buried. It was chilling.

Our days were spent going round in a lorry with our concert party entertaining different lots of troops. We were going down this road and I felt very uneasy. It was just too quiet. I said: "Stop. There's something wrong."

We got out and and we had a look round and saw a sign that said "Achtung! Minen!" that had been overgrown by the hedgerows. That road was mined with Teller mines, so there was no guarantee you could get back by going over the wheel marks you had just made. You could have hit a mine under the ground. You could hit it 10 times and nothing would happened but, on number 11, up it would go. I was petrified. But somehow we managed to get back and nothing happened.

It was hard being an entertainer in wartime. The most difficult job I ever had in my life was entertaining the remains of a tank brigade that had just had a pasting from a German Panzer Division.

There were only about 20 of them and it was the first time they had seen death. They were in shock and I was sent up there with an accordionist to go up and try to bring them out of it. It was terrible. I couldn't do it for long. I did what I could but by the time I'd finished I was in shock with them.

They were in a totally different world, they were just glazed by grief. They had just watched most of their mates blown to bits in the most awful way imaginable. It was just one of the ghastly misfortunes of war that they had suddenly found themselves completely outnumbered and outgunned.

They all knew they were lucky to be alive. And they were hardly in the mood for a comedy routine. It was very very sad indeed. A terrible waste of lives. The flower of a generation died long before their time. It was in Normandy just after the invasion. A bit frightening was that.

You had to have gags ready all the time because you would be working on a makeshift stage and suddenly shells would start landing or aircraft would be approaching. If I heard tanks going past I would say: "My God the Russians are here!" because if you didn't react quickly enough, it could kill your act.

It was in Bayeux that we thought we had found the dream billet. It was a cottage with some bunk beds upstairs and straw palliasses downstairs. It was great to have somewhere to ourselves because our sleeping habits were somewhat different to ordinary soldiers. We usually got back late after a show and some squaddies complained that we woke them up. Then they got up at the crack of dawn and woke us.

So I told my lads 'this will do for us'. Arthur came in as well. We were all desperate for a good night's rest. In the middle of the night Arthur came to me and said: "I'm being bitten something rotten". And I looked at him and he was covered in flea bites.

He wouldn't go back to his bed so we just had to wait until morning to find out what was biting him. As dawn broke we saw the cause of the problem - all the downstairs floor was covered in French tramps. And it stank to high heaven. Arthur - who was in another concert party - was so badly bitten they had to send him home.

Soon afterwards we were camped in a field outside Bayeux. I don't quite know how to explain the emotions we were all feeling. We had been through such pressure and fear and we knew that there was more, probably much more, to come.

> A soldier on guard duty failed to salute the officer.
> The officer asked him: "What are you supposed to be?"
> "I'm a bit of a guard," came the reply.
> "Well, I'm a bit of an officer," said the officer angrily.
> But the soldier was unmoved:
> "Hang about a bit and I'll give you a bit of a salute."

This young soldier was just sitting on the ground a few yards away from me. He was an ordinary young bloke in his early 20s, wondering like the rest of us, what on earth he had got mixed up in. He sat with his back against the trunk of a tree and just stared bleakly into space. Then I watched in horror as he very deliberately took his rifle, pointed at his own foot and fired. Poor chap had simply had enough, and I felt desperately sorry for the man.

Of course, officially I insisted I had seen nothing, because if such an act of obvious self-mutilation was witnessed then he would have been subjected to a very rough and ready form of discharge. I felt he deserved all the sympathy that an accidental wound on the field of battle could bring him.

I'm not branding the lad a coward, he was far from that, he had just reached the end of his personal tether. We were all under tremendous pressure. The feeling that a highly-efficient army equipped with the most up-to-date weapons of mutilation and destruction was intent on wiping you off the face of the earth does tend to concentrate the mind somewhat. People who hadn't seen what happened ran up and helped him but I just walked away. It seemed to be the only thing to do.

At moments like that I used to retreat into humour. We all tried to send little bits of money back to our families, not that anyone relying on his Army pay ever got much spare cash. One lad was desperate to send his wife something but they had run out of postal orders, so he bought two dozen penny stamps and sent them all. His wife took one look and snorted: "Here we are hard-up and he goes and sends us a picture of his blasted regiment!"

The great British strength is our ability to use humour to help fight adversity. This is never more important than in war-time. Other nations simply cannot do this. Their approach is much too serious.

We all seemed so young, I don't think the generations that followed can quite appreciate what a World War is really like. The fear and the pressure and the tension was always with you.

As a youngster I didn't like thunder and lightning. It used to frighten me silly. I didn't exactly hide under the stairs but I was always glad when it had gone. After a few weeks in Normandy listening almost hourly to a much more deadly thunderous noise of hostile shells, often too close for comfort, I lost that nervousness for good. I've never worried about thunder and lightning since. I couldn't care less about it.

The constant bombardment from the Germans - and from our artillery and the ships in the Channel - was simply something most of those of us lucky enough to survive came to terms with.

I remember one night we went into this little bar where there was entertainment. It was down in a cellar, very sleazy, just a little bar and there was a model of a bull or a cow there and the fellow pumped its tail and you got a drink. I won't say what part of the creature the drink came out of but it usually brought the house down when we watched the reaction of people getting their first drinks.

Just as you were starting to relax, a bloody great spider dropped down from the ceiling right into your drink and then flew up in the air again on some sort of elastic. It was a really weird place and no mistake.

I feel privileged to have been a member of one of those five little shows included in the Normandy landings. Whatever our show-business ambitions, we were soldiers first and entertainers second.

I was on duty one night and the Sergeant came up to me. I said: "How do?" He said: "What do you mean How do?" I said: "Do you want a drink? He shouted: "Sergeant of the Guards, arrest this man." I said: "Shut up. I've only got enough for us two."

We went over with the idea of fighting but we entertained when the opportunity arose, to keep morale up. Most of us had never been in the firing line before so you can imagine the effect.

But I have continued to have letters since I've been in Coronation Street saying 'are you the same Bill Waddington who entertained us on the beaches at Arromanches'? And I am proud to say I am.

As the campaign swung our way, we progressed through northern France to Brussels. We were in the Belgian capital for quite some time. We were there when the Germans tried to break through at Christmas time. We had drafted a couple of women into our concert party by then, and we had a soubrette singer who was a Jewish girl. The Germans broke out and tried to cut us in half through the Falais Gap. Her stories brought home the horrors of the people we were fighting and she was terrified of what would happen to her if they were successful. They weren't far off doing it but it was a determined last-ditch effort.

My mother might have been a hard taskmaster and a bit strict on my love life, but she was a very caring mother. In one of her parcels to me she had sent me a bar of Dr Lovelace's Soap, an excellent product which happily came wrapped in black and white greaseproof paper.

In Brussels we were granted a rare night off but, as usual, we hadn't got any money. Until I had a brainwave. The old £5 notes were white in those days and this greaseproof paper was printed in black and it looked a bit like a fiver.

I trimmed the wrapper down to the size of a note and carefully cleaned all the soap off it. It seems very dishonest now but I thought: "Here we are saving their lives and we can't even go and have a night out."

We went in to this hotel and I shouted: "This is an English five pounds, can I change it?" The bloke gave me 500 francs, so we had one hundred francs a piece. We had a great night out and all bought wrist watches. I didn't feel guilty, I thought: "We could all be dead tomorrow. Why not?"

In Belgium we worked at the ABC, a great big modern night club which was sheer luxury after some of the places we had worked in. We had got the Germans well out of the way then, so we used to go and have a night out there. We only had a few shillings between us. ]

There was this strange indoor whippet racing track in Brussels. You could go in this place and get a drink or a sandwich. They had to use whippets because the track was so small, greyhounds would never have got round the corners. You could have a bet like on the tote, just a few francs here and there. The owners would go and put these little dogs in the traps themselves and they would fly out for the race.

I watched quite a few times and was most amused by this old lady. She would go and put this dog in the starting trap, then go part of the way round the track and stand looking in by a window onto the course. The dog ran off fast enough but as soon as it approached its mistress, it all but stopped and wagged its tail!

I said to a pal: "The first time that woman doesn't stand by that window I'm going to back that blinking dog!" After a few races my idea came true. She went off somewhere else and we all put our money on her dog. Sure enough, without its customary distraction, the dog really burned up the track and we won a packet.

# Victory

One of our worries while we were over in France was all the reports of buzz bombs raining down on Britain from Germany. These V1 and V2 rockets were deadly things but, fortunately, the RAF managed to shoot a lot of them down. Sometimes they were even able to tip the wings so these missiles packed with explosives were turned round and sent back to Germany.

When I came back from Europe I had spent about six months overseas. The normal time was about three months but I never complained so they were happy to let me go on. I came back to England and I was in London heading for our headquarters in Chelsea to get myself a pass and a railway warrant to get back home. I was just walking out of Sloane Square Underground Station when there was this tremendous explosion and I was blown right back down the steps.

A V2 had landed only a hundred yards away. The blast was unbelievable, but I never got a scratch. When I got to the HQ which was nearby, everything was in chaos. The V2 explosion had knocked everything off the walls and papers were flying everywhere. I finished up on my hands and knees scrabbling around

This bloke with one leg shorter than the other wanted to join the Army. He was amazed after his medical when he was passed A1.
He said to the doctor: "You can't pass me A1, I've got one leg shorter than the other."
But the doctor replied: "It's all right son. The ground's not level where we're sending you."

trying to find my rail warrant.

The Sergeant there was a man called Stanley Hall. He became one of the best wig-makers in London. Years later, during one of my vainer periods, he even made a toupee for me. I thought it was very nice but my wife Lilian pointed out thoughtfully: "Take it off, you look like a poof."

After we got back from Belgium, I think I was starting to feel the effects of the War. Working as a comedian is one of those jobs where you have got to keep up a very cheery exterior. Sometimes you don't get the time to make sure you keep as happy as you might on the inside.

I really was very much in need of a rest. I had been doing so much work I was absolutely exhausted both physically and emotionally. I was at one of my lowest ebbs ever. I don't think I'd had anything approaching a proper break for 18 months.

I desperately needed some leave but when I asked, they insisted there was still a lot of entertaining to do. I pleaded for a week at home. Eventually I was granted a week's leave but after two days I got a telegram saying 'Report back'.

When I got back they said there was a choice of work for me. I could either go and entertain our troops in Northern Ireland or on the forts in the Thames Estuary. That sounded pretty much like Hobson's Choice to me. I thought for a while and then opted to go to Northern Ireland, as the comedian of the show under Jimmy Hayter, who was quite a big star in those days, as the officer in charge. He was a funny little fellow, who went on to make a lot of films and become the fruity television voice advertising Mr Kipling's exceedingly good cakes.

We were loading up at Victoria, putting all our gear in this truck ready to go over to Northern Ireland. I got out my prized ukulele, which was a a beautiful instrument. Jimmy had a uke as well but it was very different. His was only a tiny little thing.

Just as a throwaway remark I said to one of the lads doing the packing: "Here, put this with its dad!" Jimmy Hayter went crackers. He played merry hell about me insulting his uke. I said: "I was only having a bit of fun. You play the ukulele, I won't play mine. You would think it was one of your family I was talking about."

In the end we got on all right and I think they were pleased to see us over there. The troops and the locals came to see the shows. They hadn't had much in the way of entertainment. There was no television and the radio only had bad news at that time.

We did a show there in the most bizarre theatre I've ever worked in. The stage stood six foot from the floor with a solid wall at both sides and at the back. I said to this Irish stagehand: "How on earth do I get on stage? There's no wings, there no backcloth. How do I get on?"

"Just go under the stage there," he said. "And the dressing rooms are down there. Then you'll find a little ladder. Go up the ladder, open the trap door at the top and you'll find yourself on stage. And shut the trap door behind you because if you don't, and you step back, you'll kill yourself."

Now it's always important in showbusiness to make an entrance. You can do it effectively

> One of the cleverest War strategies was the time we painted the English Channel green. When the U-boats surfaced, a film of green covered their periscopes and they thought they were still safe underwater. When they got to about 100 feet in the air we used to shoot them down.

by running on from the side, or dashing up from the back of the stage. You could probably do it by being lowered down from the roof, but you most certainly can't make much a job of it by clambering out of a blessed trap door!

It could only happen in Ireland. We had planned to use a piano but decided against lugging that up with us. We settled on an accordion instead and that was difficult enough.

That tour of Northern Ireland turned into quite a marathon and, as the War in Europe ground its way towards our now-assured victory, I was again feeling ready for a rest and I hoped to be able to finish my leave. I did get away but, within a few days of getting home, I was called back again and ordered down to London to the headquarters of the Central Pool of Artists in Chelsea.

I think then the strain and the pressure of

the previous five years really hit me. My life had turned upside down two or three times since I left Lancashire. I had seen death and destruction at first hand and learned how to get laughs out of the grimmest of circumstances.

But I was suddenly at the end of my tether. I desperately needed a rest and I knew it. The endless flow of gags was beginning to look in danger of drying up and the old fizz and sparkle needed urgent recharging. Quite simply, for the moment, I had had enough. The War was virtually over in Europe. So I summoned up a more heartfelt performance than I've ever even given in Coronation Street and convinced a miserable Guards medical officer that I had really shot it. I'm still not sure exactly how much of was theatrics and how much of it was for real.

But I told him I was finished. I said I was fed-up of sleeping in communal places with hundreds of other men, of eating with them and then having to go out and be the life and soul of the party on stage. I generally played on my shattered nerves so much he sent me off down to a hospital in Epsom, Surrey for treatment.

When I arrived I was frightened that I had overdone it. The place was full of all manner of fruitcakes. There were people with all sorts of nervous complaints. I wondered if I would be able to talk my way out as easily as I talked my way in.

I knew I wasn't crackers but I also knew I needed a long rest and I couldn't see any other way of getting it. The chief psychiatrist was a lady called Harrison, who was also psychiatrist to Scotland Yard. I don't know how I compared to her other clients but I think that, at the time, I just about managed to convince her that I was near the edge of going crazy.

I'm not a hard man. I hate seeing animals suffer, let alone people, and I had seen a lot of suffering, while always trying to look on the bright side of life. Eventually all the experiences I had been through started to weigh heavily. Keeping up the jokes when some horrible things were happening was not easy. I know I'm only human and I knew I had had enough.

At first the rest and lack of the endless pressure to perform and be funny was wonderful. I slept like a baby for the first time in years. But gradually the old stories came back into my mind, coupled with a whole new range of gags that seemed to arrive in my head from nowhere.

At night in the darkened ward I would start my story-telling again, usually to a noisy audience of nocturnal chuckling. There were about 100 beds in that ward and, at night, your voice would carry a long way, especially if you've been used to entertaining troops.

The amazing thing was that in the bed opposite was a Polish airman who had been shot down. They couldn't find anything wrong with him physically but ever since it happened he had never spoken. He was still in shock and although he was apparently an intelligent man, he did not speak any English.

But after about three weeks of listening to my stories and all the lads laughing away, he began to laugh along with them. Although he had no idea of the joke, he would laugh happily away. And the

> One of our lads got German Measles. You know, just like ordinary measles, but he broke out in little swastikas.

heartening thing was that, soon afterwards, he really bucked up and he did recover. That told me an awful lot about the power of humour.

I made a lot of friends in that hospital, and one chap I really got to know well was a fellow who cleaned buses for the council called Norman Newell.

I was writing little ditties for pantomimes and he was two beds away. I had my ukulele and he said: "I would love to write songs." To try him out I told him to go away and write a song about Cinderella. I said: "I know them all so you can't kid me with someone else's."

In 20 minutes he was back. There was no music in his voice at all but the lyrics were brilliant and the basic melody was fine. I befriended him. I said: "I think you have got something." We started writing little bits of tunes. I was into song plugging in those days. I used to get £25 quid for plugging a song on the radio. It was much more than the fee for the broadcast. It was a fortune at the time.

I had a friend called Syd Coleman from Cinephonic Music and I recommended Norman to him. I said: "I've found a feller for you. Why don't you put him in a shop selling sheet music and, if someone comes in with a bad lyric, let him have a look at it?"

They gave him a job in Charing Cross Road. I knew he had talent. When he got that job he was on two-and-a-half quid a week cleaning buses. He went up to £10 or £12 straight away, which was good money then.

We kept in close touch and I said 'if anybody approaches you, Norman, talk to me first.' An American musical act called Forsyth, Singer and Farrell collared him and wanted him to sign up with them. I said: 'Don't sign anything, because they're not big enough for you.'

Whenever I was on in London I would get him to come to the show and introduce him to anyone I thought might help him. I'd say: 'Look, Dorothy Squires is on the bill, you might be able to plug her a number.' He went on to become head of Decca and head of HMV.

I did my very very best for that man. I didn't want anything in return but a Christmas card would have been nice. By the mid-50s I had had some success of my own and I called round one day to see him in my Rolls Royce. His secretary rang through to him and came back with the message that he was much to busy to see me.

I asked a psychologist years later why people should be like that. He reckoned some people who rise a long way are ashamed of their beginnings, which seems a sad lookout to me. I went to stay with his family in Plaistow. They were clean, nice people. They hadn't got a lot of money, but what does that matter? People should be proud of having started down there

> I had a terrible boil on my knee so I
> went to see the MO and asked for a
> bread poultice. "We haven't
> got any bread," I was told.
> "What about cake?" I asked.
> "No," said the MO.
> "Cake is only for officers."

and making something of themselves.

That spell of rest and recuperation soon put me right back on my feet but I had decided I had had enough of soldiering. The War in Europe was over. Germany was beaten, and I thought I had done enough - six-and-a-half years for very very little. I went in to see the discharge panel and told them I thought now was time I got out of it.

There was a Colonel on the panel who said: "What have you been doing during the War?" I thought, 'bloody hell after all I've been through.' I just said: "Oh, messing about here and there," as casually as that. He said: "Do you know who you're talking to?" I said: "No, I don't, I'm just answering a question." He just looked round and the other all nodded and I was out of the Army.

In return for risking life and limb on the

battlefields of Europe, I was handed a gratuity of just £85. It was not the greatest booking I've ever had, but perhaps one of the most eventful.

I duly went and got my demob suit. Everybody seemed to have chalk stripe suits and I wanted to be different. I got a check suit - it was hideous - and I got a trilby, Oh God, it looked as if it was made for a pet dog, it was a terrible trilby! And when I went back to my unit for my discharge they were laughing at me. I thought: 'that's good, keep laughing; that is my business now'.

When I got home my father looked at me and I said: "It's over for me, Dad." He looked back and just said: "What a bloody awful suit." I laughed and said: "Yes I'm going to give it to one of the lads in the taproom." He shouted: "That's me finished for the night, Mother," and he took his Dimple Haig bottle of whisky off the shelf where he'd saved it, sat on the stairs and drank it all neat. He never asked anybody to have a drink, he just poured it down himself.

The War in Japan was still going on, but by the beginning of 1945 it was grinding to a close. I now had to try to make my way as an entertainer without any military assistance. My firm ambition was to become a Star out of

Battle-Dress, but it was not as easy as I thought.

I was practised in the strange arts of amusing soldiers, but the paying members of the general public were quite another proposition. I knew what troops were about so I did struggle for a while. Still, I was young and determined and my success on radio helped me to get quite a few bookings.

Steadily I moved into wider-ranging, more sophisticated material and the receptions started to improve. Until I arrived in Aberdeen that was. It was scarcely a dream booking but I knew it would be good experience. And it was certainly that.

Norman Newell helped me to get my bags on the train at Euston. I had a sleeper to ease the journey north. I had been doing very well but I knew I was in a different market now, talking to Scottish audiences. I found myself some digs, in a great big granite house where my landlady's first words to me were: "Do you like kippers?" I should have known. I had kippers for every meal. I had them roasted, boiled, stewed, fried, standing up, lying down and about a hundred other ways as well.

I was busy writing a broadcast for a few week's time - in those days you had to submit

> For anyone who was not very, shall we say, regular, the Army had one all-embracing remedy, a dreaded laxative known as Number Nine. I went to the medical officer once in need of an urgent dose only to be told there had been a run on the stuff, if you'll forgive the expression. "We've run out of Number Nine," said the NCO to the MO. "Well give him four Number Two's and owe him one."

all your scripts. I was going to Dundee the following week and I certainly wasn't at my best. I went on the stage at Aberdeen and I think I really died that night. It was the only time it happened to me. The audience just didn't know what I was on about. That was totally distressing for me because I had been doing so well everywhere else.

I went back to my digs and sat and thought 'how on earth can I get past these people?' I was second top of the bill and the experience of failure upset me so much that I put cotton wool in my ears when I came off the stage so I could concentrate on my writing and not hear if anybody else did well: I couldn't stand it. It was cowardly, I know, but I had to do it to get my broadcasts finished.

I did a little bit better second house but all week I really struggled. It was awful. Until Friday night. On Friday night, I absolutely paralysed them. I got such a laugh when I went on that I thought my flies were undone. I actually stopped and turned round to make sure they weren't. I have never gone so well in my life. Second house, I paralysed them again. It was fantastic. I stuffed the cotton wool back in my ears and went off back to my digs floating about two feet above the ground. I was really elated. I thought 'I hope she has some kippers ready for me'. I tried to puzzle out what had suddenly gone right.

When I got back she said: "Are ye no going down to the docks?" I said: "What do I want to go down to the docks for?" "To see the fireworks," she said. "It's VJ Night, the Japanese have capitulated, the War's over." I didn't believe it.

Of course, that was why I had gone down so brilliantly on stage. Everyone was so relieved the War had finished and many of them had already started to celebrate. Half of them were drunk and the other half were well on the way. They were all going mad in the audience because the War was over. Next night I went back to dead silence.

And I had to carry on to Dundee the week after. That wasn't much better. And then it was

Glasgow Empire, a real graveyard for English comics if ever there was one.

But I've always learned from my experiences in life and that trip to Scotland was highly educational. I tailored my material more carefully, slowed down a lot and later did very well on my visits north of the border. That time was when I started the change. I took the mickey out of myself, I laughed at my bald head and eventually I got past them.

There was a little greasy spoon cafe behind the Glasgow Empire and I went in for a cup of tea in between shows. A man and a woman came in and started talking. There had been a Scottish comic on as well as me. He was dirty but he got some laughs. And I didn't, not to that extent.

But then I heard this woman say: "I like the little English comic. He was very good. But the other fellow wants to get his act cleaned up. I'll go and watch the English comic anytime."

That cheered me up a bit. I had seen people succeed with blue material and it had made me wonder, if that was what people wanted, maybe I should give it to them. But you have to have principles in life so I never did. I resolved that if I couldn't get laughs doing it my way, properly,

A lot of lads went to the MO to get out of going on route marches. One of them said he was having trouble with his chest. He said: "Every time I breathe in and out my chest hurts." The MO said: "All right. I'll excuse you breathing for a fortnight. Next."

then I wouldn't bother. But that woman gave me heart.

As the War was finally finishing I got the boost to my new career that I really needed. It came after a show at Southend-on-Sea, of all places. I had done my usual turn, complete with customary heavy white make-up and daft outfit. It went well enough but afterwards the opinion of the all-powerful Cissy Williams, the chief booker for Moss Empires chain of theatres, was relayed to me.

Cissy's verdict was: "He's not quite ready for us yet, and he doesn't need all that make-up." I took the tip to heart.

My next date was at the Bedford Theatre, Camden Town, as the comic on the bill with Ivy Benson and her Girls' Band. That afternoon I went down the Charing Cross Road in London and bought myself a smart suit and a trilby at Cecil Gee's. The outfit cost me £36 and it was the best investment I ever made in my life. For the first time I went on stage just as myself without any funny make-up, joke moustaches or silly props. And even though I say it myself, I paralysed them. I went down a bomb. I couldn't believe that I was going down so well.

The bar after the show was packed with agents and I booked five years work. My new career was off and running. And that time I didn't have a hint of scrumpy or anything else to help me. This time I was stone cold sober.

**The Sergeant Major's ill in bed, he really has gone through it. They told him where to put his rifle, damn fool tried to do it.**

The next time I went to Glasgow Empire, I was prepared. It still had the deadly reputation. Poor old Des O'Connor walked on the stage and collapsed, fainted. He just couldn't work there, he was frightened to death. And Jimmy James arrived on the train from London, stepped onto the platform and said: "My God it's been a long week."

But I went back just after the War and did well.

In a funny way the War was a fantastic opportunity for me. It gave me the chance to step from nowhere right up on stage and start entertaining people.

It was an exhilarating apprenticeship into showbusiness. If it had not been for the War, it would have taken me a lot longer to get going.

In one way you couldn't have it rougher as a comedian than trying to crack jokes to soldiers who have just seen their mates killed or performing on Carpiquet Airfield with a foot of a dead German poking up through the earth.

And yet it was such a unique and emotive experience. We were young men who knew we were fighting with right on our side. I never asked to get taken out of the frontline and pushed into a battle to get laughs. But once it happened, I believed totally in the importance of what we were doing.

Morale is vital to a fighting force and I was given the chance to work to improve that morale by using the powerful weapon of humour, to bring out strength through adversity. I am proud to have lifted a few spirits at important times.

And although I've seen some sad sights, and I can never forget that this book is dedicated to the men and women of the Allies who lost their lives, most of my memories of wartime as happy and positive.

In these modern, materialistic times days it

is not always fashionable to dwell on the old days. But the comradeship I found in World War Two was so warm and impressive to me that I don't think I will ever quite cool down.

Faced by a common enemy of unparalleled evil, the British people got together in the most heart-warming and unselfish way possible. Decency and camaraderie were cherished, not derided, and I am very proud to have been a minute part of those times.

It still seems remarkable to come all the way through the Normandy Landings without a scratch while thousands of men lost their lives. Standing in the British Cemetery in Bayeux, I am not at all ashamed to say the old tears were welling up.

I've had 50 marvellous years of life since those lads were so cruelly slain. Half a century of experience that was viciously denied to thousands of brave soldiers.

This book is my humble salute to them.